potatoes

from pancakes to pommes frites

potatoes

from pancakes to pommes frites

Annie Nichols

photography by Peter Myers

RIZZOLI
NEW YORK

Dedication

To Winnie and Fred Nichols, my mum and dad, for a
childhood full of wholesome food, especially Dad's
new potatoes—the best in the west.

My thanks to Dave and Allan, Pete and Sean Myers,
Wei Tang, the gang at Backgrounds, Becky Johnson for
her enthusiastic assisting, and also to Marwan Badran,
his mother Leonora and his aunt Rainie for their
generous help with the Iraqi recipes.

Thanks also to Jennifer John and Hazel Jenkins of the
British Potato Council and Wendy Jenkins of
The National Potato Promotion Board
7555 E. Hampton Avenue, No. 412
Denver, Colorado 80231
Tel 303.369.7718, Fax 303.369.7718

First published in the United States of America in 1998 by
RIZZOLI INTERNATIONAL PUBLICATIONS, INC.
300 Park Avenue South, New York, NY 10010

First published in Great Britain in 1998 by
Ryland Peters & Small
Cavendish House
51–55 Mortimer Street
London W1N 7TD

Art Director **Jacqui Small**
Art Editor **Penny Stock**
Designer **Lucy Hamilton**
Editor **Elsa Petersen-Schepelern**
Photography **Peter Myers**
Food Stylist **Annie Nichols**
Stylist **Wei Tang**
Indexer **Hilary Bird**
Production **Kate Mackillop**
Author Photograph **Catherine Rowlands**

ISBN 0-8478-2077-7
LC 97-69574

Printed and bound in Hong Kong

contents

There are hundreds of different varieties of the potato, and each country has developed types suitable for local climatic and market conditions. In America, the four basic categories —russet, long white, round white, and round red—can be divided further as follows, based on their suitability for different culinary uses.

Floury potatoes (far right) are wonderful for baking, French fries, and deep-frying. Varieties include Russet Burbank (also known as Idaho.)

Waxy varieties (front), such as Round White and Round Red, can be boiled, served whole in salads, mashed, roasted, or fried, but are less suitable for baking.

All-purpose varieties include Yukon Gold, with golden to buttery yellow flesh—which is best boiled or mashed—and Long Whites, which are slightly denser than the floury Russets.

New potatoes (rear), with thin, flaky skins, are simply the young form of any potato (baby Long Whites, for instance, are known as Finger Potatoes). New potatoes should be used within a few days of purchase, and are best boiled or pan-roasted. They are now available all year round.

Special "gourmet" potatoes include unusual blue varieties which range from blue-black to lavender-purple, and very interesting red-fleshed varieties. All are wonderful simply boiled and tossed in butter, chopped herbs, and seasonings.

potato
varieties

boiled and steamed
potatoes

Mashed potatoes, salads, and crushes

Boiling and Steaming

New potatoes should be added to salted boiling water—full-size potatoes should be put in cold salted water then brought to a boil. Steaming takes a little longer than boiling. Boil or steam potatoes of similar size together to ensure they cook evenly. Don't pierce to test for tenderness until towards the end of the cooking time, or the potatoes will absorb water, become soggy, and fall apart.

Most of the nutrients are just under the skin of the potato, so leave the skin on when boiling, and peel only when cooked. Peeled potatoes also absorb more water during cooking.

Take care peeling hot potatoes—hold them in a clean cloth, or leave until cool enough to handle, then reheat as necessary.

Mashed Potatoes

Soft, fluffy, and creamy—mashed potato is the epitome of comfort food. It can be served as a side dish, as a dish in its own right, or used as the basis for many other dishes, such as croquettes or potato cakes. People like different kinds of mashed potato—from coarse and lumpy, to light and fluffy, or an almost pourable consistency. Choose floury potatoes for the best texture in mashed potatoes. Waxy potatoes produce a lumpy mash, known as a crush. Potatoes cooked in their skins retain nutrients and have a dry texture which takes liquids and flavorings better. If boiling peeled chunks of potato, drain when cooked, return to the pan, and allow to steam dry for a few minutes.

Mash with a potato masher for a coarse texture, or press through a food mill (see page 96) for a fluffy, light texture. A good result can also be achieved with a potato ricer—like a giant garlic press (see page 50). Sieving, pressing through the fine blade of a meat grinder, or careful use of a hand-held electric mixer will also give good results. When mashed, beat well with a wooden spoon or a strong wire whisk.

Do not, under any circumstances, use a food processor, or you will end up with something that looks like wallpaper glue! For a lighter texture, heat liquids such as milk or cream before beating in.

If using the mash to make piped potato toppings and garnishes, add beaten egg yolk to produce a glazed, golden color.

Classic Mashed Potato Recipe

Scrub 2 lb. medium-size floury potatoes, then boil in lightly salted water for 20 to 30 minutes until tender. Drain, cool, and peel, then mash with 1 stick butter. Reheat, season, then beat in 1¼ cups hot milk.

New Potato Crush Recipe

Boil 1 lb. small waxy or new potatoes until tender, then crush lightly with a fork. Season, then stir in butter or olive oil to taste.

Flavored Mashes

The basic, delicious mashed potato can be flavored with any number of herbs, spices, vegetables, and other ingredients.

Olive Oil Mash

Mash boiled potatoes with warmed olive oil, salt, pepper, and (optional) hot cream and grated Parmesan cheese—delicious, and also healthier than potatoes mashed with butter.

Saffron Mash

For a fragrant, bright yellow mash, add saffron to the water when boiling peeled potatoes, or infuse the saffron in milk or cream before adding the liquid to the mash.

Pesto Mash

Add 2 tablespoons pesto to plain mash.

Herb Oil Mash

For strong flavor and bright color, purée parsley (shown left), basil, chives, mint, cilantro, or other soft herbs with olive oil in a food processor, then add to the mash.

Garlic Mash

Roast garlic cloves, squeeze the flesh out of their skins, crush them well, then stir them into the mashed potato.

Cheese Mash

Stir in grated Parmesan or a melting cheese such as fontina or Gruyère, or a crumbled blue cheese such as Gorgonzola.

Mustard Mash

Add 2 tablespoons whole-grain mustard.

Other Mashes

Stir in puréed parsnips, celeriac, sweet potato, rutabaga, turnip, beets, salsify, pumpkin, artichokes (globe or Jerusalem), cabbage and other greens, fennel, celery, mushrooms (wild or cultivated—porcini are especially good), eggplant, leeks, or roasted onions. Try spices and flavorings such as nutmeg, horseradish, truffle, olive tapenade, sun-dried tomatoes, chile, sweet bell peppers, nuts (raw or roasted, then ground), lemon, orange, chopped or puréed apple, sweetcorn, arugula, watercress, mashed anchovy, or a cream of salt cod.

oven-cooked
potatoes

**From roasting
to baking—
from gratins
to pies**

Roasting Potatoes

The perfect roast potato has a crisp, crunchy surface and a soft, fluffy interior. Floury varieties are the best for roasting, though small waxy potatoes are also used in some cuisines, notably modern Italian. Roast potatoes with onions (either whole or cut into wedges), garlic cloves in their skins, thyme, or rosemary for extra flavor. If roasted with meat, the result will be less crisp, but will have excellent flavor.

Preparation

Potatoes can be roasted with or without their skins, but if peeled and cut into chunks, the pieces should be uniform, so they cook at the same rate. Par-boiling first gives a softer interior and crisper edge. After par-boiling, put them back in the pan and swirl them around to roughen the edges or, holding each one in a clean cloth, score the surface with a fork.

Oils and Fats

The oil or fat used to cook potatoes is a matter of taste and regional tradition. Olive, vegetable, canola, or peanut oils are now the most common choice, largely for health reasons. However duck and goose fat are famous for giving the most wonderful flavor. Lard and drippings, now rarely used, also give very good flavor.

Roasting Method, Times, and Temperatures

Put oil or fat in a roasting pan large enough to hold the potatoes in a single layer. Heat on top of the stove or in the oven. Add the potatoes to the hot oil (take care in case the oil sputters). Season, then turn to coat with oil. Roast in a preheated oven at 425°F for 1 hour, turning occasionally, until crisp on the outside and tender inside. The time depends on the size of the potatoes.

Baking Potatoes

Potatoes baked whole have a fluffy interior with a crispy skin. Serve smaller ones with broiled or roasted meats. Larger ones are served on their own, slit lengthwise, and filled with flavorings ranging from simple cold butter to cheese, beans, or canned tuna. Floury varieties are best.

Preparation

Scrub the potatoes and prick with a fork. A metal skewer can also be pushed into each potato. For a crunchy crust, roll the wet potatoes gently in sea salt before baking.

Baking Method, Times, and Temperatures

Place the potato directly on the oven shelf or wrap the potato in foil. Bake at 400°F for 1 to 1¼ hours or until soft in the center when tested (or, if using a skewer, when it can be easily removed). To cook a large number at once, increase heat to 425°F.

Microwaving

Baking in a microwave will not give the crisp skin that results from oven-baking, but is a very quick method if you're in a hurry. Prick the potato all over with a fork, place on a piece of paper towel, and microwave on high for 8 to 10 minutes (15 minutes for 2 potatoes, about 20 to 25 minutes for 4 potatoes), or until the potato is tender when tested. Let stand 2 to 3 minutes before using. Baking times vary according to the oven wattage and the size, shape, and variety of the potatoes.

Potatoes Baked in the Coals

This potato baking method is popular in Australia. As part of a beach or garden barbecue, whole potatoes are placed in the coals of a (wood-fired) barbecue. To serve, the black, ash-covered skins are broken open, then sea salt and a spoonful of butter or olive oil is added.

Potato Wedges and Potato Skins

Cut the potatoes into wedges, brush with olive oil, then season well, and cook at 400°F for 20 to 25 minutes, turning them over once or twice.

To make potato skins, bake in the usual way, then cut into wedges lengthwise. Scoop out the flesh (use for another purpose) leaving some attached to the skin. Brush the skins with oil and roast or deep-fry until crisp and golden. Drain on paper towels and serve warm with a dip.

Gratins and Pies

To make a gratin, potatoes are layered in a dish with cream, milk, or butter, then topped with cheese and/or breadcrumbs, and baked until the top is crisp and golden, and the center is creamy. Other vegetables, especially root vegetables, can be layered alternately with the potato.

Dishes such as fish pies, shepherd's pies, and cottage pies are fish, lamb, or beef stews respectively, topped with mashed potato, then baked until lightly golden. A vegetarian version can be made with a vegetable ragout topped with a layer of mashed potato, then baked.

Sautéed Potatoes

This is one of the classics of the French culinary repertoire. Raw potato is sautéed gently in fat such as butter, oil, a mixture of the two, duck or goose fat, clarified butter, lard, or bacon fat mixed with oil, then served sprinkled with flakes of sea salt.

Deep-fried Potatoes

Floury potato varieties are best. Use a deep-fryer or large, deep pan, and never use oil at a depth of more than one-third to a half full. A wok, third full of oil, is also good—you can move the potatoes around so they cook evenly. Always reheat oil to the required temperature between batches, and lower the potatoes gently into the oil to prevent splashing. A frying basket, wire scoop, or slotted spoon allows the potatoes to be turned and lifted easily. Do not overcrowd the pan, or the heat will be reduced and the potatoes will boil rather than fry, absorb too much oil, and become greasy and soggy. Fry at 350–375°F. If fried at too low a heat, the potatoes will absorb too much oil; if too high, they will burn.

Oils and Fats

Peanut or corn oil cook at a high heat without burning. Olive oil is wonderful but extravagant. Sunflower oil, safflower oil, and lard are also used. Always use clean oil, strain after use, and when re-using, remember what was cooked in it previously (to avoid fishy tastes!)

Safety First!

Always dry the potato well, as excess water makes the oil sputter and boil. Never leave the pan unattended, and clean up any spills immediately. Turn the handle away from the edge of the stove so it can't be bumped. If the oil starts to smoke, turn off the heat immediately. In the event of a fire, turn off the heat and cover the pan with a lid, baking tray, or a thick, damp cloth. Do not move the pan or use water to extinguish the fire. Let the pan cool completely before moving it.

Deep-fried Fries

Perfect fries are twice-cooked. Cut potatoes into long strips ¼ to ½ inch thick, rinse well in cold water to remove the starch, then dry well. Fry in hot oil at 325°F for 5 minutes until tender but pale, then drain well. Raise the heat to 375°F and cook again for 1 to 2 minutes until crisp and golden. Check temperatures with a deep-frying thermometer or test-fry a cube of bread: it will turn golden in 1 minute at 350°F or in 40 seconds at 375°F.

Potato Chips

Very thinly sliced potatoes, rinsed of starch, then patted dry, are deep-fried until crisp and golden. These are best cut on a mandolin (see page 137)—useful and efficient for finely slicing vegetables. It has a wooden, metal, or plastic frame with a set of adjustable cutting blades; smooth for slicing and cutting chips, or fluted for cutting gaufrettes and straw potatoes. The best have a protective guard between you and the vegetables, so you don't cut yourself. Mandolins can be expensive, but cheaper plastic Chinese and Japanese brands are sold in oriental shops. (Even top chefs use them!)

Pommes Soufflés

Slice thin rounds of potato on a mandolin, then twice-fry as for fries, so they puff up like a soufflé.

Gaufrettes or Waffle Potatoes

Using a mandolin, slice the potato once on the fluted cutting blade, then turn the potato 90° and slice again to produce a finely latticed slice. Deep-fry until crisp and golden.

Straw Potatoes (Matchsticks)

Julienne very finely, then deep-fry.

Potato Ribbons

A variation on straw potatoes (see page 43 for the cooking method).

Potato Baskets

Potato baskets are made by lining a wire basket with unrinsed, very thinly sliced potatoes, then pressing a smaller wire basket inside. The whole thing is deep-fried until crisp. Special utensils are available, but a simple substitute can be made with large and small sieves that fit snugly together.

Croquettes and Fritters

Balls, rounds, or ovals of mashed potatoes are coated with flour, egg, and breadcrumbs, polenta, chopped nuts, or crushed vermicelli, then deep-fried.

sautéed and deep-fried potatoes

From fries to rösti—
from chips to croquettes

the
americas

South America was the original homeland of the potato. It was taken to Europe by Spanish and English adventurers, then by the Portuguese to West Africa and Asia. Pre-Columbian Americans cultivated **hundreds of varieties**, and even more still grow wild.

These little stacks of tostadas are usually made with corn tortillas, but they are wonderful made with potato wafers as a modern alternative.

tostadas

crispy potato tostadas
with salmon and scallop seviche

---

1 lb. salmon fillet, carefully deboned with tweezers

8 small scallops, or larger ones, sliced crosswise (roe removed)

1¼ cups freshly squeezed lime juice

⅔ cup freshly squeezed orange juice

⅔ cup freshly squeezed lemon juice

1 red chile, seeded and very finely chopped

1 small red onion, very thinly sliced

½ avocado, peeled and chopped

2 tomatoes, peeled and chopped

2 tablespoons chopped fresh cilantro, plus sprigs to serve

2 tablespoons extra-virgin olive oil

salt and freshly ground black pepper

Potato Wafers:

1 lb. potatoes

¼ cup butter, melted, plus extra for greasing

salt and freshly ground black pepper

Serves 4

Slice the salmon as thinly as possible. Place all the fish slices in a shallow non-metallic container. Mix the lime, orange, and lemon juices together and pour over the seafood. Cover and chill for 4 to 6 hours.

To make the potato wafers, grate the potato finely, but do not wash. Drain in a sieve, then wrap the potato in a clean cloth and squeeze well to extract the moisture. Put the potato in a bowl, stir in the butter, and season with salt and pepper. Mix well, then divide the mixture into 12 portions.

Lightly grease a baking tray with butter. Put a 4½-inch pastry cutter on the tray and spoon one portion of the grated potato mixture inside the ring. Spread evenly with the back of a teaspoon. Lift the ring and repeat with the remaining mixture to make 12 wafers. (You may need 2 trays.)

Put the sheet or sheets in a preheated oven and bake at 400°F for about 5 to 6 minutes. Remove from the oven and turn the wafers over with a spatula. Return to the oven and continue baking for a further 3 to 4 minutes or until both sides are golden brown and crispy.

Make sure the fish is completely opaque, indicating that it is "cooked." Thirty minutes to 1 hour before serving, drain off the liquid and carefully stir in the chile, onion, avocado, tomato, chopped cilantro, and olive oil. Season and set aside.

To make one serving, put a potato wafer on a small plate. Top with a little of the fish mixture, top with another potato wafer, followed by more fish mixture and a final potato wafer, until you have a 5-layered tower. Repeat to make 4 servings altogether, garnish with cilantro sprigs, and serve.

Though creamy mayonnaise-style sauces are the traditional dressings for cold potato salads, modern American chefs have been experimenting successfully with highly flavored dressings based on extra-virgin olive oil, now known to be the healthiest form of oil. Potatoes have a special affinity with strong flavors.

roasted warm potato salad

2 lb. small new or salad potatoes
½ cup extra-virgin olive oil
sea salt flakes
I small red onion, finely chopped
8 black olives, pitted and finely chopped
1 ½ tablespoons capers,
rinsed and drained
6 sun-dried tomatoes in oil,
drained and chopped
5 tablespoons chopped
fresh flat-leaf parsley
I tablespoon balsamic vinegar
freshly ground black pepper
Serves 4 to 6

Place the potatoes in a roasting pan, add 2 tablespoons of the olive oil, sprinkle with sea salt, and toss well to coat.

Bake in a preheated oven at 400°F for 25 to 30 minutes, or until tender, turning the potatoes occasionally.

While the potatoes are roasting, combine all the remaining ingredients in a large bowl, mix well, and season with salt and pepper.

Remove the potatoes from the oven, crush each potato slightly with a fork, and cut in half. Toss the still-warm potatoes in the bowl of dressing, and serve either warm or cold.

Variation:

To make Blue Potato Salad, boil or roast the potatoes in their skins until tender—the time will depend on the variety, age, and size of the potatoes. Serve tossed in butter and chopped herbs (optional). Purple or black potatoes are best served in the same way, so their extraordinary color can be best appreciated.

Variation:
Blue Potato Salad
2 lb. blue, purple, or black potatoes
8 tablespoons butter
salt and freshly ground black pepper
chopped herbs (optional), to serve

gingered seafood chowder
with red roe cream and poppyseed crackers

Potatoes are native to South America, so it is hardly surprising that some of the most exciting potato recipes come from the Americas. Chowders are typical New England soups—the New World versions of fishermen's stews such as *bouillabaisse* and *bourride*. Vital ingredients include potatoes and bacon, and usually seafood of some kind, though chowders can also be made with chicken, or for vegetarians. Clam chowders are traditional, but shrimp and scallops can also be used, and are equally delicious.

3 tablespoons butter
2 thick bacon slices, cut crosswise into small strips
1 onion, chopped
1 small garlic clove, crushed
1-inch piece fresh gingerroot, peeled and finely grated
1 tablespoon all-purpose flour
4 cups milk
1 lb. potatoes, cut into ½-inch cubes
1 bay leaf
8 oz. fresh scallops with roes, whites cleaned and sliced horizontally into 2 to 3 pieces if large (reserve the roes)
2¾ cups light cream
12 uncooked jumbo shrimp, peeled and deveined
chopped chives and parsley, to serve
Poppyseed Crackers:
1⅔ cups all-purpose flour
a pinch of cayenne pepper
1 teaspoon sugar
1 teaspoon salt
2 tablespoons butter, diced
1 tablespoon poppyseeds, finely ground in a spice or coffee grinder
⅔ cup whole milk
sea salt flakes
Serves 4

1 To make the poppyseed crackers, sift the flour, cayenne, sugar, and salt into a large bowl. Rub in the butter until the mixture resembles fine breadcrumbs. Stir in the poppyseeds. Slowly add the milk to form a soft but firm dough.

2 Divide the dough in half and roll out to 2 large rectangles, 12 x 16 inches each. Trim the edges, then transfer to a lightly greased baking tray or trays. Score the surface into 2-inch squares and sprinkle with a few sea salt flakes.

3 Bake in a preheated oven at 400°F for 6 to 8 minutes until golden. Turn the pieces over with a spatula and cook 5 to 6 minutes longer. Transfer to a wire rack, let cool, then break the crackers apart.

4 To make the chowder, melt the butter in a large stockpot, add the bacon and cook until crisp. Add the onion, garlic, and ginger and sauté gently for 5 to 10 minutes until softened and translucent but not colored.

5 Add the flour. Cook, stirring, about 2 minutes without coloring. Stir in some milk until smooth, then add the remainder. Add potatoes and bay leaf, simmer 8 to 10 minutes until tender, remove from the heat and season to taste.

6 Measure 4 tablespoons of the cooking liquid into a small pan, bring to a simmer, add the red scallop roes, and cook for 30 seconds or until just firm. Remove from the heat and purée roes and liquid in a small blender until smooth.

7 Reserve about 4 tablespoons of the puréed roes and pour the remainder into the chowder. Add the cream, and bring slowly back to a boil. Add the shrimp and cook for 1 minute—no longer or they will overcook.

8 Add the scallops and cook for a further minute. Serve the chowder in individual bowls, sprinkled with the herbs, drizzled with the reserved red roe purée, and accompanied by the poppyseed crackers.

This traditional French cooking method has been adopted enthusiastically by modern American chefs. Cooking in a package means all the flavor and goodness of the potatoes is retained as they cook in their own steam. Open the packages at the table to relish the wonderful aromas rising from the potatoes. New potatoes are best used as soon as possible after purchase—good supermarkets renew their supply after only 2 to 3 days to avoid spongy, wrinkled potatoes that are past their prime.

potatoes en papillote
scented with fresh herbs

Cut out 4 sheets of parchment paper, 12 x 15 inches each, and fold in half lengthwise.
Draw a large curve in the shape of half a heart.
Cut on the line and open the paper.
Place a quarter of the potatoes on one half of each piece of paper. Dot the butter evenly over the potatoes, sprinkle with sea salt, and add a herb sprig to each.
Brush the edges of the paper lightly with the beaten egg and fold over. Starting from the rounded end, pleat the edges together in small folds so that each parcel is completely sealed. Twist the final ends together. Place the parcels on a baking tray and bake in a preheated oven at 400°F for 25 to 30 minutes until the packages are well puffed with steam and the potatoes are tender (open one of the parcels to test.)
Serve immediately.

1 lb. very small new potatoes
¼ cup unsalted butter
4 sprigs fresh herbs such as thyme, tarragon, chervil, mint, or rosemary
sea salt
1 large egg, beaten
Serves 4

empanaditas

Empanadas are pastry turnovers popular in Spanish and Latin American cooking. They usually have savory fillings, but can also have a fruit filling and be served as a dessert. Usually baked or deep-fried, they can be either very large, or a smaller variety, known as *empanaditas*. Serve them on their own, or with a spicy fruit salsa made of papaya, mango, peaches, or pineapple mixed with red onion and chile. Salsas are a spicy, fashionable Mexican contribution to the world's culinary repertoire.

2 medium potatoes, cut in ¼-inch dice
3 scallions, chopped
¾ cup canned corn kernels, drained
1 or 2 green chiles, seeded and finely chopped (optional)
3 oz. ricotta or goat cheese, crumbled
1 tablespoon chopped fresh marjoram
½ teaspoon paprika
salt and freshly ground black pepper
Pastry:
1⅔ cups all-purpose flour
½ teaspoon salt
7 tablespoons butter, melted
2 to 2½ tablespoons water
vegetable oil, for deep-frying
Makes 16

empanaditas

1 Parboil the potatoes in a saucepan of lightly salted boiling water for 2 to 3 minutes, drain well, and let cool. Combine the remaining filling ingredients in a bowl, stir in the potatoes, season with salt and pepper, and set aside.

2 Sift the flour and salt into a large bowl, stir in the butter, and add enough water to form a soft but firm dough. Knead briefly, wrap in plastic wrap, and leave to rest for 30 minutes at room temperature.

3 On a lightly floured surface, roll out the dough to ⅛-inch thick, then cut out 16 rounds, 5 inches in diameter, using a small saucer as a guide. Knead and re-roll any trimmings. Place 1 tablespoon filling on each round, a little off-center.

4 Dampen the edges of the pastry with a little water and fold in half over the filling. Using the tines of a fork, press the edges together to seal them. Place the *empanaditas* on a tray and refrigerate for about 30 minutes to 1 hour.

5 Fill a deep pan ⅓ full of oil. Heat to 375°F or until a cube of bread browns in 40 seconds. Fry the *empanaditas* in batches, turning once, for about 3 to 5 minutes, or until golden brown. Drain on paper towels and serve.

The baked potato, roasted whole in its skin, then split and topped with a variety of delicious fillings, is a great American staple that has been adopted enthusiastically in other parts of the world. In this version the flesh is scooped out of the shells, mixed with beaten egg and other ingredients, then spooned back into the shell and baked again. The result is a sublime fluffy filling.

american baked potato
with fluffy soufflé fillings

4 large baking potatoes

sea salt flakes

1 tablespoon butter, diced

⅓ cup milk

2 large eggs, separated

salt and freshly ground black pepper

Smoked Salmon Filling (shown left):

3 oz. smoked salmon, cut into strips

2 tablespoons chopped fresh chives

1 tablespoon capers, rinsed, drained and coarsely chopped

4 sun-dried tomatoes in oil, drained and finely chopped

Anchovy Gruyère Filling (variation):

8 anchovy fillets, mashed with a fork

4 oz. Gruyère cheese, cut in ¼-inch dice

2 tablespoons chopped fresh flat-leaf parsley

10 black olives, pitted and finely chopped

Serves 4

Wash the potatoes thoroughly, shaking off most of the water. Prick them all over with a fork and sprinkle with sea salt flakes. (This is optional but gives a wonderful crispy crust.) Bake in a preheated oven at 400°F for about 1 hour or until cooked through. Reduce the oven temperature to 350°F.

In a bowl, combine your chosen filling ingredients and reserve. While the potatoes are still hot, cut off a ½-inch slice lengthwise and discard, or reserve for another purpose. Using a spoon, scoop out the flesh, leaving a ¼-inch shell. Push the scooped-out flesh through a potato ricer, food mill, or sieve into a large bowl. Place the shells on a baking tray. Add the butter to the potato flesh and mix well to incorporate. Heat the milk to just below boiling point, then beat into the potato mixture. Beat the egg yolks and add to the potato, mixing well. Stir in the filling mixture and season to taste with salt and pepper. Beat the egg whites until stiff but not dry. Fold in a third of the beaten egg whites to loosen the mixture, then gently fold in the rest.

Spoon the mixture back into the shells, heaping the tops. Bake on the tray in the oven for 15 to 20 minutes until slightly risen and lightly browned on top.

I found this delicious tart in New Mexico. The chile kick is quite subtle—roasting the chiles softens the flavor. Potatoes are great partners for the verve of chiles, and you can also add chiles to the pastry for added zest.

chile potato tart
with roasted tomatoes and garlic

1½ lb. ripe red plum tomatoes, halved lengthwise and seeded

3 tablespoons extra-virgin olive oil

4 whole garlic cloves, unpeeled

1 large red chile

1½ teaspoons sea salt flakes

1 tablespoon sugar

1 lb. waxy potatoes, boiled in their skins for 15 minutes, then peeled and sliced thinly

1¼ cups crème fraîche, lightly whipped and seasoned with salt and pepper

salt and freshly ground black pepper

Chile Pastry:

1⅓ cups all-purpose flour

a pinch of salt

7 tablespoons unsalted butter, diced

¼ cup finely grated Parmesan cheese

1 red chile, seeded and very finely chopped (optional)

Serves 6

To roast the tomatoes, lightly brush a baking tray with some of the olive oil and arrange the tomatoes cut side up. Add the garlic and whole chile and sprinkle with the remaining olive oil.

Sprinkle the salt and sugar evenly over the tomatoes and bake in a preheated oven at 350°F. Remove the garlic after 10 to 15 minutes when soft, and squeeze the flesh into a bowl. Remove the chile after 15 to 20 minutes when the skin is blistered and slightly charred. Leave the tomatoes for 45 to 50 minutes until very soft and slightly charred. Cool the chile a little, then peel, seed, chop finely, and add to the garlic. Scoop the tomato flesh into the bowl, discarding the skins. Mash the flesh with a fork. Season to taste.

To make the pastry, sift the flour and salt into a bowl. Rub in the butter until the mixture resembles fine crumbs. Stir in the Parmesan and chile, if using. Add enough cold water to make a firm dough, then roll out on a lightly floured surface and use to line a greased, 10-inch fluted tart pan. Lightly prick the base with a fork. Chill for 30 minutes, then line with foil and baking beans. Heat a baking tray on the middle shelf of a preheated oven at 400°F. Put the tart shell on the tray, bake for 10 to 15 minutes, then remove from the oven and remove the foil and beans. Increase the oven heat to 450°F.

Spread the tomato mixture evenly on the tart base, then cover with concentric circles of potato slices. Pour the crème fraîche over the potato. Bake for 8 to 10 minutes until the top is golden.

These little fried cakes of potato and chorizo with a crisp corn salsa are based on a dish I found in Mexico. *Queso fresco* is a mild fresh cheese often used in Mexican cooking. I have substituted fresh goat cheese, which has an affinity with spicy food though it isn't traditional. You could also use a feta cheese, as long as it is not too salty.

tortitas

tortitas de papa
with chorizo and corn salsa verde

1½ lb. potatoes, unpeeled, scrubbed well
3 chorizo sausages, peeled and crumbled
1 garlic clove, crushed
4 scallions, chopped
8 oz. goat cheese, crumbled
1 large egg, beaten
salt and freshly ground black pepper
½ cup fine dry breadcrumbs
olive oil, for cooking

Corn Salsa Verde:
1 tablespoon Dijon mustard
1 tablespoon lime juice or wine vinegar
⅔ cup extra-virgin olive oil
2 tablespoons capers, rinsed and chopped
½ cup canned corn kernels, drained
2 scallions, finely chopped
1 or 2 garlic cloves, chopped very finely
6 tablespoons chopped fresh flat-leaf parsley
6 tablespoons chopped fresh cilantro
1 or 2 green chiles, finely chopped
sea salt and freshly ground black pepper

Serves 6

Put the potatoes in a large saucepan, bring to a boil, then simmer for 15 to 20 minutes or until tender. Drain well and, when cool enough to handle, peel and pass through a potato ricer, food mill, or a sieve into a large bowl.

Heat a non-stick skillet, add the chorizo, and sauté gently for 5 to 10 minutes until the fat renders. Lift out the chorizo with a slotted spoon, let it cool slightly, then add to the bowl of potato. Add the garlic, scallions, and goat cheese and mix. Add the egg, salt, and pepper and mix well.

Divide the mixture into 18 parts and form into small flat cakes. Roll each potato cake in the breadcrumbs, pressing gently so the crumbs stick. Set aside while you make the salsa.

To make the salsa verde, put the mustard in a small bowl and beat in the lime juice or wine vinegar. Continue beating, adding the olive oil in a thin stream until amalgamated. Stir in the remaining ingredients, then add salt and pepper to taste.

Heat a thin layer of oil in a large skillet and sauté the potato cakes in batches until golden brown all over (about 8 to 10 minutes). Drain on paper towels and keep them warm while you cook the remaining potato cakes.

Serve with the salsa and a crisp salad, such as the mizuna, arugula, and baby spinach leaves shown here.

This American classic is named after the deep dish in which it is cooked. An American chef taught me this version with fluffy potato pastry.

chicken pot pie
with porcini mushrooms and potato pastry

2 sprigs tarragon

I free-range chicken (3–4 lb.)

3 carrots, chopped

2 celery stalks, chopped

I bay leaf

a few parsley stalks

I onion, chopped

Porcini Filling:

½ oz. dried porcini mushrooms

I tablespoon butter

2 onions, chopped

4 slices pancetta or streaky bacon, cut into small strips

I tablespoon all-purpose flour

2 tablespoons lemon juice

⅔ cup heavy cream

2 tablespoons chopped tarragon

salt and freshly ground black pepper

Potato Pastry:

I cup plus 2 tablespoons all-purpose flour

a pinch of salt

6 tablespoons butter, diced

¾ cup mashed potato

I large egg yolk, beaten

Serves 4

Push the tarragon into the chicken and place in a large stockpot with the carrots, celery, bay leaf, parsley stalks, and onion. Cover with 8 to 12 cups of water, bring to a boil, then simmer gently for I hour until the vegetables are tender.

Transfer the chicken to a plate and cool slightly. Strip the meat from the chicken and separate into evenly sized pieces. Divide the meat between 4 small pie dishes. Strain the stock into a clean pot, discarding the vegetables and herbs. Bring to a boil and simmer until reduced by half.

Put the porcini in a bowl, pour over I cup of boiling water, soak for 20 minutes, then drain, reserving the liquid. Chop the porcini finely. Strain the reserved liquid through coffee filter paper set over a measuring cup. Add stock to make 2¾ cups, reserving remaining stock for another use.

Melt the butter in a skillet, add the onions and porcini, and cook gently for about 3 minutes. Add the pancetta or bacon and cook for 2 to 3 minutes to soften the onion and lightly color the bacon. Add the flour and cook without browning for I to 2 minutes. Gradually add the stock, stirring until thick and smooth. Add the lemon juice, cream, and tarragon, bring to a boil, season to taste, then remove from the heat. Let cool slightly, then portion into the pie dishes.

To make the pastry, sift the flour and salt into a bowl, then rub in the butter until the mixture resembles fine crumbs. Mix in the potato to form a soft but firm dough. Roll out to ¼-inch thick then cut 4 rounds slightly larger than the pie dishes. Brush the edges of the dishes with water then cover with a pastry lid. Trim the edges, roll out any excess pastry, and use to decorate. Make a small steam hole in the center of each pie and brush the tops with beaten egg yolk. Bake in a preheated oven at 400°F for 15 minutes, reduce heat to 350°F and bake for a further 15 to 20 minutes or until the pastry is crisp and golden brown.

Cajun cooking, from America's South, is a combination of French and Southern cuisines—full of wonderful, complex, spicy flavors. Commercial Cajun spice mixes are widely available, but I prefer the homemade quality of the flavorings in this recipe, with fresh onion and garlic, as well as the spices and herbs added separately.

cajun potato wedges
with spicy lemon and onions

4 potatoes, unpeeled,
cut lengthwise into 4 or 6 wedges

I lemon, cut into 6 wedges

8 whole garlic cloves, unpeeled

2 red onions, cut lengthwise through
the root end into small wedges

4 or 5 bay leaves

3 tablespoons freshly
squeezed lemon juice

4 tablespoons water

I tablespoon tomato purée

½ teaspoon freshly ground black pepper

I teaspoon salt

I teaspoon paprika

½ teaspoon cayenne pepper

I teaspoon dried oregano

I teaspoon dried or fresh thyme leaves

½ teaspoon ground cumin

4 tablespoons olive oil

Serves 4

Bring a large saucepan of lightly salted water to a boil. Add the potato wedges, bring back to a boil, and cook for 3 minutes. Drain well and place in a large roasting pan with the lemon wedges, garlic, onions, and bay leaves.

Combine the lemon juice, water, and tomato purée in a small bowl. Add the spices and herbs and mix together well.

Pour the spice mixture over the potatoes in the pan and toss together to coat.

Drizzle over the oil and cook in a preheated oven at 400°F for 35 to 40 minutes, or until the potatoes are tender and all of the liquid has been absorbed. Turn the mixture frequently with a metal spatula. Serve hot with broiled meats.

One of the world's best-known potato dishes, in which potatoes—mashed, grated, or cubed—are cooked slowly in oil, bacon fat, or butter. Use a cast-iron pan to ensure slow, even cooking. The artichokes are not traditional, but they are utterly delicious!

hash browns

3 lemons (2 squeezed, I halved)

12 baby artichokes*

6 tablespoons olive oil or clarified butter (or a mixture of both)

4 garlic cloves, finely sliced

I tablespoon fresh thyme leaves

I lb. floury potatoes, boiled in their skins, then peeled and cut into ½-inch dice

salt and freshly ground black pepper

Serves 4

Variation:

Classic Hash Browns

I small onion, finely chopped

6 tablespoons clarified butter or olive oil

I½ lb. cooked floury potatoes, peeled and cut into ½-inch dice

salt and freshly ground black pepper

*If using artichokes bottled in oil, cook the garlic briefly until softened, then add the artichokes, thyme, and potatoes and continue as in the main recipe.

Pour the lemon juice into a bowl large enough to hold all the artichokes and half-fill the bowl with cold water. Cut off the artichoke stems I inch from the base of the globes. Slice off the pointed tops of the globes. Remove 2 to 3 layers of outer leaves to expose the tender yellow leaves, then rub the cut surfaces with the halved lemon and put the artichokes in the bowl of acidulated water. If the artichokes are large, scoop out the hairy center chokes with a teaspoon and discard. One by one, remove the artichokes from the water, cut finely lengthwise into ⅛-inch slices, then replace in the water. When ready to cook, drain well.

Heat the oil or butter in a large heavy-based skillet. Add the garlic, thyme, and artichokes, cover, and cook gently, stirring occasionally, for 6 to 8 minutes or until just tender.

Add the potatoes, spreading evenly over the pan. Season, then cook over low heat for 15 to 20 minutes. Press down frequently with a spatula, shake the pan occasionally, and cook until the base is crisp and golden. Cover the skillet with a large plate or tray, flip over, then slide the hash browns back into the skillet. Cook the other side, pressing down, until golden and crisp. Serve for breakfast with broiled fish or meat.

Variation:

Classic Hash Browns

Sauté the onion in the butter or oil until softened, then add the potatoes and seasoning, and proceed as in the main recipe.

europe

Elizabethan heroes **Drake** and **Raleigh** have been credited with introducing the **potato** to Europe from South America, while Irish immigrants took it back to North America in the 1700s. **Parmentier** made it fashionable in France, where some potato dishes are now called *Parmentier* in his honor.

fish and chips
tuna strips with potato ribbons

There can be no dish more British than traditional fish and chips—and it is also popular in former British colonies around the world. The batter should be light, the chips (fries) should be thick-cut and twice-fried to delicious crispness (see page 12). Ideally, they should be sprinkled with salt and vinegar, wrapped in newspaper, and eaten sitting on the sea wall in a fishing village in Scotland.

This recipe is a modern update of the great classic. Tuna, the king of fish, is not caught in British waters, but makes a great alternative to the usual cod. These curled potato ribbons are a delicious variation on traditional chips, and do not need to be twice-fried.

2 lb. floury potatoes, peeled

1 lb. piece fresh tuna

sea salt

vegetable oil, for frying

Lemon and Sesame Mayonnaise:

1 large egg yolk

1 tablespoon fresh lemon juice

½ teaspoon Dijon mustard

⅔ cup vegetable oil

1 teaspoon sesame oil (optional)

finely grated zest of 1 small lemon

salt and freshly ground black pepper

Sesame Batter:

½ cup sesame seeds

2 large egg yolks

2 cups ice water

1⅔ cups all-purpose flour,

plus extra for dusting

Serves 6 to 8

To start the batter, first put the sesame seeds in a dry skillet over low heat and cook, tossing continuously, until they are golden brown (be sure they don't burn). Transfer to a large plate to cool.

To make the mayonnaise, combine the egg yolk, lemon juice, and mustard in a food processor and pulse until blended. Combine the vegetable and sesame oils and, with the motor running, add the oil in a slow, thin stream. When the mayonnaise is thick, scrape into a bowl, and stir in the lemon zest, salt, and pepper.

To make the potato ribbons, cut each potato into ½-inch slices. Using a potato peeler, peel around the edges of each slice to form long strips. Cut off 3-inch lengths of the strips, tie into knots or bows, and place in a bowl of cold water. Alternatively, cut around the whole potato as you would peel an apple to form whole long strips.

Cut the tuna into ½-inch slices and cut the slices into thin strips, ½-inch wide. Rinse and drain the potato ribbons 2 to 3 times, then dry well with paper towels. Fill a pan or deep-fryer ⅓-full with oil and heat to 375°F or until a cube of bread browns in 30 seconds. Deep-fry the potato ribbons in batches for 3 to 4 minutes until crisp and golden.

Drain well on paper towels, sprinkle with salt, and keep warm.

To complete the batter, put the egg yolks in a large bowl, add a little of the ice water, mix well, then beat in the remaining water. Add the flour and sesame seeds and stir with a fork until just mixed. Don't worry if it is slightly lumpy—it is better under-mixed than over-mixed.

Reheat the oil to 375°F. Put a little flour on a plate, then dip each strip of tuna into the flour, shaking off any excess. Dip into the batter, then deep-fry the strips, a few at a time, turning occasionally, for 2 to 3 minutes until the fish is tender and the batter is crispy and lightly golden. Drain on paper towels and serve immediately with the potato ribbons and the sesame mayonnaise.

Antoine Parmentier, a military pharmacist, popularized the potato in France in the early 1700s. The French were suspicious of this new American vegetable, so Parmentier posted guards around his fields during the day, leaving it unprotected at night. Needless to say, the potatoes were stolen and soon became both popular and fashionable.

potage parmentier
with parsley oil and croûtons

¼ **cup unsalted butter**

1 lb. floury potatoes, peeled and sliced very thin

1 onion, sliced thin

1 bay leaf

4 cups milk

salt and freshly ground black pepper

Parsley Oil:

3 oz. fresh flat-leaf parsley, washed and dried

½ **cup extra-virgin olive oil**

Bacon-flavored Croûtons:

3 tablespoons olive oil or 2 tablespoons unsalted butter

4 slices pancetta or rindless streaky bacon

2 slices bread, crusts removed, cut or broken into ½-inch pieces

Serves 4

To make the parsley oil, bring a saucepan of water to a boil, add the parsley, and blanch for 5 to 10 seconds. Drain and refresh in plenty of cold water. Drain well, then squeeze dry in a clean cloth. Chop the parsley and put in a blender. Add the olive oil and purée until very smooth. Either use as is, or strain first through a fine sieve, then again through 2 layers of cheesecloth or a paper coffee filter. Pour into a clean bottle and use within 1 week.

To make the soup (*potage*), melt the butter in a large, heavy-based saucepan, add the potatoes and onion, stir, cover, and cook without coloring for 5 to 8 minutes, stirring occasionally, until the onion is softened and translucent.

Add the bay leaf, milk, salt, and pepper, bring to a boil, reduce the heat, cover, and simmer for 15 to 20 minutes. Remove from the heat, discard the bay leaf, pour into a blender, and purée until smooth. Strain through a very fine sieve into a clean pan.

To make the croûtons, heat the oil or melt the butter in a large skillet over moderate heat. Add the pancetta or bacon and sauté for 5 to 6 minutes until crisp. Remove with a slotted spoon and drain on paper towels. Add the bread to the pan and sauté, turning frequently, until crisp and golden. Drain on paper towels. Reheat the soup, season, and serve, drizzled with the parsley oil. Drop the croûtons and bacon into the soup or serve separately.

Pillow-soft potato pancakes make the perfect accompaniment for *gravad lax*, a favorite Scandinavian dish. The word means "buried salmon" in Swedish, but other fish can also be used, such as trout, herring, or the mackerel used here. The potato pancakes are also a wonderful breakfast or brunch dish, served with bacon, eggs, or as an accompaniment to meat or fish.

gravad lax

potato pancakes
with mackerel gravad lax

Mackerel Gravad Lax:

2 tablespoons coarse sea salt

2 tablespoons brown sugar

2 teaspoons white peppercorns, crushed

1 bunch fresh dill, chopped

6 large mackerel fillets, about 8 oz. each

Dill Cream:

1 cup crème fraîche

2 tablespoons Dijon mustard

2 teaspoons superfine sugar

6 tablespoons chopped fresh dill

sea salt and freshly ground black pepper

Potato Pancakes:

1 lb. floury potatoes

3 eggs, beaten, plus 2 egg whites, beaten

⅓ cup self-rising flour

½ cup hot milk (just below boiling)

freshly grated nutmeg

sea salt and freshly ground black pepper

corn oil or clarified butter, for cooking

sprigs of dill and frisée, to serve

Serves 6

To make the gravad lax, mix the salt, sugar, peppercorns, and dill in a bowl. Divide a third of this mixture between three large pieces of foil, sprinkling the herbs down the middle. Using tweezers, remove the bones from the fish. On each sheet, place one fillet on top of the herbs, skin side down, then sprinkle with another third of the herb mixture. Place a second fillet on top of the first, skin side up. Sprinkle with the remaining herbs and fold the foil into a package.

Place the packages on a deep-sided tray, place a board or a second tray on top, then weigh down with heavy cans or weights. Marinate in the refrigerator for 24 to 36 hours. When ready to serve, gently wash off the herb mixture and pat the fillets dry. Cut into slices slightly thicker than smoked salmon.

Mix all the ingredients for the dill cream. Set aside.

To make the pancakes, boil and peel the potatoes, then pass through a potato ricer. Let cool completely, then mash in the eggs and flour. Beat in the milk, nutmeg, and seasoning. Stir a third of the egg whites into the batter, then fold in the rest. Heat the oil in a non-stick skillet, and drop in spoonfuls of the mixture. Cook for 2 to 3 minutes on each side until golden. Drain on paper towels. Serve the pancakes with the mackerel, dill cream, dill sprigs, and frisée.

gnocchi

potato gnocchi
with walnut and arugula pesto

The success of gnocchi depends on lightly mixing the potato and flour to the right consistency—smooth and slightly sticky. If you over-mix or are heavy handed, the gnocchi will be heavy too.

My friend's mother, who taught me this recipe, has a special secret ingredient —a slosh of grappa!

Serve the gnocchi with a tomato or meat sauce, or pesto made with basil, dried tomatoes, or this unusual combination.

Arugula Pesto:

2 oz. trimmed arugula leaves, roughly chopped

¼ cup chopped walnuts

2 garlic cloves

½ cup extra-virgin olive oil

¼ cup freshly grated Parmesan cheese, plus extra to serve

sea salt and freshly ground black pepper

Gnocchi:

1½ lb. large floury potatoes, unpeeled

¾ cup all-purpose flour, plus extra for rolling

salt, to taste

Serves 4

1 To make the pesto, combine the arugula, walnuts, and garlic in a blender or food processor and process until finely chopped. Add the olive oil and blend well to form a purée.

2 Scrape the mixture into a bowl and stir in the Parmesan. Taste and adjust the seasoning with salt and freshly ground black pepper. Set aside to develop the flavors while you make the gnocchi.

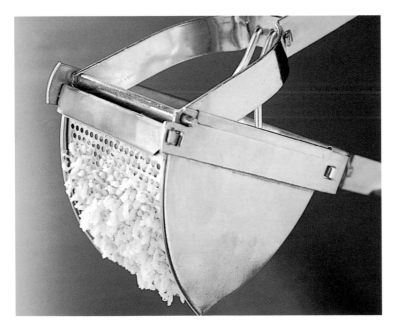

3 Put the potatoes in a pan with cold salted water to cover. Bring to a boil and cook for 25–30 minutes, until soft. Drain well, cool, then peel. While still warm, press through a potato ricer or food mill into a bowl.

4 Beat the flour into the potatoes, a little at a time. Stop adding flour when the mixture is smooth and slightly sticky (the moisture in the potatoes will vary according to their age and variety). Season with salt to taste.

5 Turn out the mixture onto a well-floured board, then roll out the dough into long sausages about ¼ inch in diameter. Cut each sausage into short pieces about 1 inch long.

6 Place each piece on the end of your thumb and press the prongs of a fork lightly over the top. The pieces will be hollow on one side and grooved on the other. Drop them onto a floured plate as you make them.

7 Bring a large pan of water to a boil and add 20–25 pieces at a time. They will quickly rise to the surface. Let them cook for 10–15 seconds longer, then remove with a slotted spoon and put in a bowl while you cook the rest.

8 Add the pesto to the bowl and gently turn the gnocchi in the mixture, until they are well covered. Take care not to break them. Serve immediately with extra Parmesan cheese.

The idea for this simply delicious recipe comes from my Italian friend Daniela. It is *pizza al trancio,* the Italian takeaway snack usually found in bakeries where slices are heated up for you (*trancio* means "slice"), and one slice is placed on top of the other with the filling in the middle, to be eaten like a sandwich.

pizza con le patate

Pizza Dough:

1 cake fresh yeast, or 1 tablespoon or 1 sachet active dry yeast

a pinch of sugar

¾ cup warm water

2½ cups white bread flour

2 tablespoons olive oil

½ teaspoon salt

Herbed Potato Topping:

1 lb. waxy potatoes, peeled and sliced thin

2 tablespoon extra-virgin olive oil

4 garlic cloves, crushed

leaves from 2 sprigs rosemary

1 teaspoon sea salt flakes

Makes two 10-inch pizzas

To make the pizza dough, place the yeast and sugar in a small bowl and blend together well. Mix in the warm water and leave for 10 minutes or until frothy.

Sift the flour into a large bowl and make a well in the center. Pour in the yeast mixture with the olive oil and salt. Mix together to form a soft but firm dough. Tip out onto a lightly floured surface and knead the dough for 10 minutes until smooth.

Divide the dough in half and form into balls. Place the dough balls on a floured work surface or tray in a warm place and sprinkle them liberally with flour. (This will become the base of the pizza and will make it easier to slide onto the tray.) Let rise for about 1 hour or until doubled in size.

Put 2 baking trays in a preheated oven at 425°F until hot. Combine the potato slices, olive oil, garlic, rosemary, and salt in a large bowl and toss together to coat.

Brush off any excess flour from the top of the dough, then turn the balls upside down on a work surface, and roll and pull each one out to a large circle about 10 inches in diameter. Spread the potato mixture evenly over both pizzas. Remove the trays from the oven and slide 1 pizza onto each one. Sprinkle with more olive oil and salt if required and bake for 15 to 20 minutes until the potatoes are tender and the pizza is lightly golden and crisp.

rösti

swiss rösti

A Swiss classic. I once worked as a chef in Switzerland, and I cooked rösti hundreds of times. These soft buttery pancakes topped with wild mushrooms are reminiscent of a dish I tasted one summer high in the Swiss Alps. My friend Stephan has an 84-year-old grandmother who picked the wild mushrooms from the forests in the surrounding valleys. Rösti can also be served topped with fried eggs, sprinkled with Gruyère cheese, or served separately with meat and sausages.

2 lb. potatoes, unpeeled and well scrubbed
¾ cup clarified butter *
1 onion, chopped
4 oz. pancetta or bacon, cut into thin strips
1 lb. wild mushrooms or large, flat, cultivated mushrooms, or a mixture of both, cut in halves or quarters if large
2 tablespoons chopped fresh flat-leaf parsley
sea salt and freshly ground black pepper
Serves 4

*To clarify butter, melt over a gentle heat, then let cool. Pour off and keep the pure butter and discard the solids.

1 Put the whole potatoes in a large saucepan and cover with cold water. Bring to a boil, and cook for 10 to 15 minutes until just tender. Drain well, let cool slightly, peel, then grate coarsely into a large bowl.

2 Heat 2 tablespoons of the butter in a skillet, add the onion and bacon, and cook for 5 to 6 minutes until the onions are softened. Tip this mixture into the bowl of potato, season with salt and pepper, and mix well.

3 Heat half the remaining butter in a skillet, add the potato mixture, and press down slightly to form a large pancake. Cook for 10 minutes, adding a little extra butter around the edges, and shaking the skillet occasionally.

4 Carefully cover the skillet with a plate and flip over. Add more butter, then slide the rösti back in to cook the other side. Add more butter around the edge and cook until golden, about 7 minutes. Remove from heat and keep warm.

5 Heat the remaining butter in a skillet. Add the mushrooms and sauté, stirring occasionally, for 3 to 5 minutes until tender but still firm. Season with salt and pepper and stir in the chopped parsley.

6 Serve the rösti topped with the mushrooms. You can also divide the rösti mixture in 4 before cooking to serve as a small starter—or vary the topping according to taste, and garnish with a few peppery salad leaves.

This method of cracking the potatoes and cooking them in red wine comes from Cyprus. Cooked slowly with coriander seeds, the potatoes absorb all the wonderful juices.

patates spastes

cracked new potatoes
in coriander and red wine

2 lb. small new potatoes, unpeeled, scrubbed, and dried

4 tablespoons olive oil

1 tablespoon coriander seeds, crushed well

salt and freshly ground pepper

⅔ cup red wine

4 tablespoons chopped fresh cilantro leaves

Serves 4 to 6

Put the potatoes in a clean cloth and, using a wooden mallet or other heavy kitchen implement, thump the potatoes to crack them open. (Don't be over-zealous or you will end up with raw mashed potato!)

Gently heat the oil in a skillet large enough to hold the potatoes in a single layer. Add the potatoes, coriander seeds, salt, and pepper and cook, turning the potatoes occasionally, until lightly golden all over. Add the red wine, let it boil, then reduce the heat, cover the pan, and simmer gently, shaking the pan occasionally, for 15 to 20 minutes, or until the potatoes are tender.

Remove from the heat and stir in the chopped fresh cilantro leaves. Serve as an accompaniment to meat or poultry.

A wonderful creamy gratin of waxy potatoes layered with spinach, herbs, Gruyère, and crème fraîche. It can be served hot or cold, and makes an easily transportable picnic dish.

potato gratin
with herbs, spinach, and cheese

I garlic clove, crushed

I tablespoon unsalted butter, melted

I lb. trimmed fresh spinach

3 large eggs, beaten

2¼ cups crème fraîche

1¼ cups grated Gruyère cheese

2 oz. chopped fresh herbs, such as chives, parsley, chervil, or sorrel

a pinch of freshly grated nutmeg

a pinch of cayenne pepper

salt and freshly ground black pepper

2½ lb. large waxy potatoes, peeled

To Serve:

salad leaves, such as shin joi, red chicory (endive), or red shiso

vinaigrette, to taste

sea salt and cracked black pepper

Serves 6 to 8

Mix the garlic and melted butter together and use to grease a deep 9-inch springform cake pan.

Wash the spinach and place in a large pot with just the water that is left clinging to the leaves. Cover and heat, stirring once, until the spinach has just wilted. Drain well and squeeze out any excess moisture. Chop finely.

Beat the eggs with the crème fraîche, stir in the chopped cooked spinach, and two-thirds of the Gruyère. Add the herbs and season well with nutmeg, cayenne, salt, and pepper.

Slice the potatoes thin.

Cover the base of the cake pan with a layer of potatoes and spread evenly with a spoonful of the cream and spinach mixture. Continue layering, finishing with a layer of potatoes. Sprinkle with the remaining Gruyère cheese and herbs, then cover the pan with a piece of foil.

Place the filled çake pan in a roasting pan and fill the pan with enough boiling water to come half way up the sides. Carefully place in a preheated oven and bake at 350°F for about 1½ hours or until the potatoes are tender—test by piercing the center with a knife or skewer. Remove the foil for the last 15 minutes to allow the top to brown.

Turn out onto a plate and serve hot or cold with salad leaves drizzled with vinaigrette and sprinkled with sea salt and lots of cracked black pepper.

potato soufflé
with mozzarella and almond-parsley pesto

Each spring, summer, and fall, I teach at the excellent Tasting Places cookery school in Sicily, and I was shown this Italian recipe by Carla Tomasi, one of my fellow chefs at the school.

A soufflé of hot, fluffy potato with nuggets of mozzarella and fontina cheese melting delectably through the mixture—it is the epitome of comfort food.

Serve the soufflé with this wonderfully scented pesto of roasted almonds and parsley puréed with the finest extra-virgin olive oil for a perfect accompaniment to salad as a lunch or supper dish.

Almond Parsley Pesto:
I bunch flat-leaf parsley, washed and stalks removed
¹/₃ cup almonds with skin on, toasted in the oven until very golden, then cooled
I cup extra-virgin olive oil
¾ cup grated Parmesan cheese
salt and freshly ground pepper

Potato Soufflé:
3 tablespoons unsalted butter, melted
½ cup dry breadcrumbs
3 lb. floury potatoes, unpeeled, boiled in lightly salted water for 30 minutes, or until very soft, then drained and peeled while still hot
¼ cup unsalted butter, at room temperature
⅔ cup milk, warmed
2 large eggs, plus I large egg yolk
½ cup freshly grated Parmesan cheese
4 oz. mozzarella cheese, well drained and cubed
4 oz. fontina or Emmental cheese, cubed

Serves 4

1 Grind the parsley, toasted almonds, and 2 tablespoons olive oil to a fairly coarse texture in a mortar and pestle or food processor. Scrape into a bowl, then stir in the remaining oil and Parmesan cheese, and season to taste.

2 Before making the the soufflé, generously grease a 9-inch soufflé dish or cake pan with half the melted butter and coat well with half the breadcrumbs, shaking out any excess.

3 Mash the hot potatoes through a potato ricer or food mill, or push through a sieve. Add the butter and warm milk and mix well. Beat the eggs, add to the mixture, and season well. Add the Parmesan and mix well again.

4 Spoon half the potato mixture into the prepared soufflé dish or pan, pushing it up against the sides. Drop in the cheese cubes, spreading them out slightly, then cover with the remaining potato mixture.

5 Brush with the remaining butter and sprinkle with more breadcrumbs. Bake in a preheated oven at 350°F for 20 minutes, then increase the heat to 425°F for 10 minutes until a golden crust has formed on the top.

6 Serve from the dish or spooned onto a serving plate, with salad and pesto. **Note:** The uncooked soufflé can be prepared 2 days in advance and refrigerated in its dish, but bring back to room temperature before baking.

When mixed with wheat flour, or even made into potato flour, potatoes produce wonderful texture in baked goods. Pastry made with potato, for instance, is light and crumbly; potato bread has a delicious moist crumb; and shortbread made with a percentage of potato flour has a fine texture.

kartoffelkrapfen

potato turnovers
with chicken livers

2 lb. floury potatoes, unpeeled
¼ cup unsalted butter
2 large eggs, beaten
salt and freshly ground black pepper
1 cup self-rising flour
1 teaspoon caraway seeds
⅓ cup fine dry breadcrumbs
Chicken Liver Filling:
¼ cup unsalted butter
1 onion, finely chopped
1 celery stalk, finely chopped
1 carrot, finely chopped
1 lb. chicken livers, trimmed
½ teaspoon paprika
1 tablespoon tomato purée
4 tablespoons chopped fresh parsley
½ cup white wine or chicken stock
salt and freshly ground black pepper
Makes 16 to 18

Place the potatoes in a large saucepan of salted water, bring to a boil, and simmer for about 30 minutes or until soft. Peel the potatoes while still warm and pass through a potato ricer or food mill, or push through a sieve into a large bowl. Beat in the butter, one of the beaten eggs, salt and pepper, then gradually knead in the flour and caraway seeds until well mixed.

Turn the potato mixture onto a well-floured work surface and roll out to ¼ inch thick. Let cool completely.

To prepare the filling, melt the butter in a skillet. Add the onion, celery, and carrot and cook until softened and lightly golden. Raise the heat, add the chicken livers, and cook, stirring frequently, until sealed all over. Stir in the paprika, tomato purée, chopped parsley, and wine or stock, season with salt and pepper, and let cool.

Cut the potato dough into rounds 5 inches in diameter and place 1 tablespoon of filling in the center of each. Fold over and press the edges firmly together. Arrange on a greased baking tray, brush with the remaining egg, sprinkle with breadcrumbs, and bake in a preheated oven at 400°F for 20 to 30 minutes until golden. Serve as a snack, or as a light lunch with salad.

Salt cod was a traditional export from Scandinavia to Catholic Europe and even to the Caribbean. It appears, with potatoes in the dishes of many countries, from the *brandade* of France to the *baccalá* of Venice.

portuguese fish fritters
with Greek skorthalia

1 lb. salt cod fillets

1 lb. floury potatoes, unpeeled, scrubbed well

1 small onion, finely chopped

2 tablespoons chopped fresh flat-leaf parsley

1 large egg, lightly beaten

freshly ground nutmeg

salt and freshly ground black pepper

⅓ cup all-purpose flour

vegetable oil, for deep-frying

Greek Skorthalia:

1 cup fresh white breadcrumbs

¾ cup ground almonds

4 garlic cloves, crushed

1 to 2 tablespoons freshly squeezed lemon juice

⅔ cup extra-virgin olive oil

salt and freshly ground black pepper

Makes 32

Put the fish in a bowl of water and chill for 24 to 36 hours, changing the water 2 to 3 times. Drain, rinse, and place the fillets in a pan of cold water. Bring to a boil, then simmer for 5 to 10 minutes until tender. Drain, cool a little, remove the skin and bones, then flake the flesh into a bowl and mash with a fork. Cook the potatoes in a large saucepan of salted water for 15 minutes until just tender. (Do not test before this time or the potatoes will be very soggy.) Drain, cool a little, then peel and mash the flesh well, preferably with a food mill or potato ricer. Mix the potatoes into the fish, then add the onion, parsley, egg, nutmeg, and pepper. Add salt to taste. Divide into 32 walnut-sized balls, place on a tray, cover, and chill for 30 minutes. Sprinkle the flour on a large plate. Roll each fish ball lightly into the flour, shaking off any excess, then set aside.

To make the skorthalia, put the breadcrumbs in a bowl, cover with water, soak for 5 minutes, then squeeze out the excess liquid. Put in a blender or food processor, add the almonds, garlic, and 1 tablespoon lemon juice. Process briefly until mixed. With the motor running, gradually add the olive oil in a very thin steady stream until the mixture resembles mayonnaise. Scrape into a bowl and season with salt, pepper, and more lemon juice to taste.

Fill a deep pan ⅓ full of oil and heat to 375°F or until a cube of bread browns in 30 seconds. Add the fish balls a few at a time and deep-fry for about 2 minutes, turning occasionally until golden all over and cooked through. Serve hot with the skorthalia for dipping.

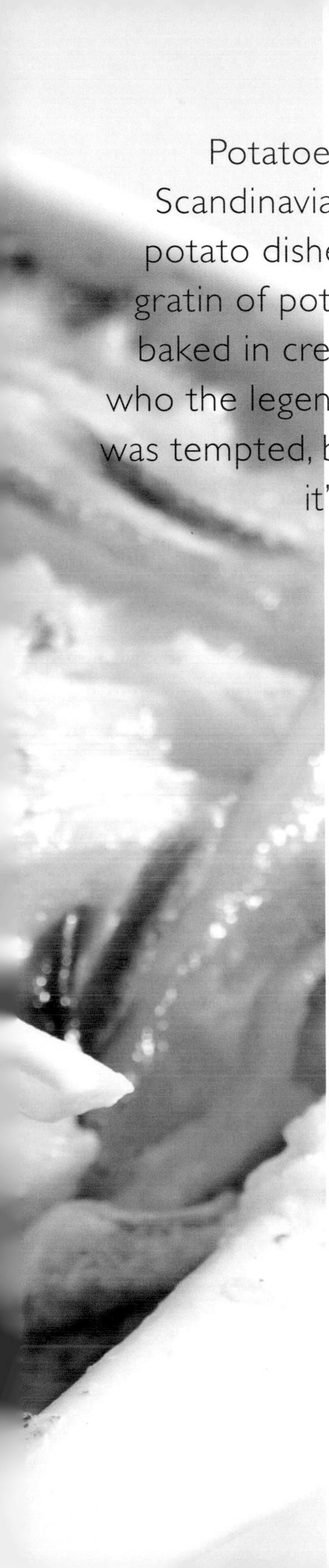

Potatoes thrive in cold climates, and Scandinavia is the source of many great potato dishes. This is the classic Swedish gratin of potatoes, anchovies, and onions baked in cream. Nobody seems to know who the legendary Jansson was, or why he was tempted, but this recipe is so delicious it's no wonder he succumbed!

jansson's frestelse

jansson's temptation

¼ cup unsalted butter

2 large onions, thinly sliced

2 lb. waxy potatoes, peeled

16 to 24 anchovy fillets in olive oil *

2 cups light cream

sea salt and freshly ground black pepper

Serves 4

*If possible, use the less salty Swedish anchovies, or white anchovies, usually sold in jars.

Grease a gratin dish, about 13 x 9 inches, with a little of the butter. Melt half the remaining butter in a pan, add the onions, and cook for about 10 minutes or until softened and golden. Cut the potatoes into matchstick-sized pieces—this is easiest using a mandolin, but otherwise use the small cutting disk on a food processor, or simply cut with a knife.

Layer the potatoes, onions, and anchovies into the gratin dish, starting and ending with potatoes. Criss-cross the anchovies as you go, and season between the layers.

Dot with the remaining butter and bake in a preheated oven at 375°F for 10 minutes. Open the oven, pour over half the cream and return to the oven for a further 10 minutes. Pour over the remaining cream and bake for about 20 to 30 minutes or until the potatoes are tender and golden brown.

Hasselbacks are perhaps the best-known of all Swedish potato recipes. The original uses butter and breadcrumbs, and sometimes Parmesan, and bay leaves are a favorite Scandinavian herb. The potatoes are sliced almost to the base, so the slices open out like a fan when cooked, and the edges become crispy and golden.

bay-roasted hasselbacks

24 small potatoes, unpeeled, well scrubbed

approximately 20 fresh bay leaves, torn in half lengthwise

1 tablespoon unsalted butter

3 tablespoons olive oil

1 or 2 garlic cloves, crushed

sea salt flakes and freshly ground black pepper

Serves 4 to 6

To prepare the potatoes, place 2 chopsticks on a board and lay a potato lengthwise between them. Using a sharp knife, and holding the sticks and potato in place, make crosswise cuts ⅛ inch apart, cutting just down to the sticks. Alternatively, spear each potato lengthwise with a skewer about ¼ inch from the base, slice across as described above, then remove the skewer.

Insert a couple of pieces of bay leaf, or a whole bay leaf if small, in each sliced potato. Melt the butter with the olive oil in a heavy-based roasting pan. Over moderate heat, stir in the garlic, and carefully add the potatoes in a single layer. (Take care, they may sputter.) Move them around for 2 to 3 minutes to color slightly, then season with sea salt flakes and freshly ground black pepper. Place the pan in a preheated oven at 375°F and roast for 25 to 30 minutes until the potatoes are golden brown and tender. As they cook, the potatoes will open out like a fan.

Serve as an accompaniment to meat or poultry, or with baked cod or roasted salmon.

Pure comfort food, champ and colcannon are an inextricable part of Irish childhood memories. Dip each forkful of potato in the little pool of butter before eating. Blue cheese, especially Irish Cashel Blue, is my own optional addition!

champ

1½ lb. floury potatoes, peeled

10 scallions, including the green tops, chopped

1¼ cups milk

¼ cup butter, plus extra for serving

7 oz. blue cheese, crumbled (optional)

salt and freshly ground black pepper

Serves 4

Cut the potatoes into large, even dice and boil in salted water for about 20 to 25 minutes or until tender. Drain well. Put the scallions in a saucepan with the milk, bring to a boil, then simmer for 2 to 3 minutes. Remove from the heat and set aside to infuse for 10 minutes.

Mash the potatoes using a potato ricer or food mill, beat in the milk and scallion mixture, then the butter, salt, and pepper. Pour into a clean pan and reheat gently. To serve, spoon into small bowls in mounds, make a hollow in the top, and insert more butter and cheese (if using).

Variations:

Colcannon (shown left), Ireland
Kale, cabbage, or another leafy green vegetable is used instead of the scallion and cheese. It is served in the same way as champ, or formed into little cakes and sautéed in butter to form a crunchy crust.

Clapshot, Scotland
Follow the recipe for champ. Omit the scallion and cheese. Add 1½ lb. boiled, mashed rutabagas. Chopped scallions, chives, or bacon fat may also be added.

Kailkenny, Scottish Highlands
Follow the recipe for colcannon, adding ½ cup cream.

Rumbledethumps, Scottish Borders
1½ lb. each of cooked potatoes and cabbage are thumped (mashed) then rumbled (mixed) with pepper and 1 stick butter, topped with cheese, and broiled brown.

Punchnep, Wales
Half-and-half mashed turnips (neps) and potatoes are heaped into a mound and studded with hollows, which are then filled with cream.

champ

potatoes dauphinoise

Two of the finest French potato dishes are *gratin dauphinois* and *pommes à la dauphinoise*. They are very similar, but in the latter sliced potatoes are baked with cream and garlic. (I prefer to roast or boil the garlic first for a more subtle flavor, but use crushed raw garlic if you prefer.) To make *gratin dauphinois* pour a mixture of eggs, milk, and cream over the sliced potatoes, then top with cheese before baking. The two names refer to the eastern French province of Dauphiné, which stretches from Savoy to Provence, rather than the *dauphine,* the wife of the former French crown prince (the *dauphin*).

4 garlic cloves
¼ cup whole milk
2 cups heavy cream
2 lb. floury potatoes, peeled
sea salt and
freshly ground white pepper
butter, for greasing
Serves 4

pommes à la dauphinoise

1　Drop the garlic into a small pan of boiling water, reduce the heat, and simmer for 20 minutes until very tender. Remove, then crush well to a purée using a mortar and pestle, or rub through a fine sieve.

2　In a saucepan, combine the puréed garlic with the milk and cream, season very well, bring to a boil, then remove from the heat.

3　Grease a roasting pan or dish measuring about 6 x 10 inches, or cake pan about 9 inches diameter. Cut the peeled potatoes into ¼-inch slices and arrange in 6 or 7 layers in the pan.

4　Pour in the cream mixture and press the potatoes down. The cream layer should come just under the top potato layer. Cook in a preheated oven at 325°F for 1½ to 2 hours, pressing the potatoes down gently every 20 minutes.

5   The cream will be absorbed gradually and the potatoes will become compressed and more solid as they cook. If there appears to be too much liquid, remove some with a spoon. When the top is colored, stop pressing.

6   Test with a knife to be sure if the potatoes are cooked. Remove from the oven and let set in a warm place for 10 minutes. Spoon straight from the dish or cut out shapes with pastry cutters for a more elegant serving.

This is a variation on the French classic potato dish *Pommes Anna*—the potato cooks down to form a solid cake that melts in the mouth. When I first worked as a chef, I used a traditional copper *Pommes Anna* mold, but I find that an ovenproof cast-iron skillet or cake pan works just as well.

pommes voisin

2 lb. waxy potatoes, peeled
6 tablespoons butter, melted
½ cup freshly grated Parmesan cheese
sea salt and freshly ground black pepper
sprigs of thyme, to serve (optional)
Serves 4

Variations:
Pommes Voisin with Jerusalem Artichokes
add to the above ingredients:
13 oz. Jerusalem artichokes
juice of 1 lemon
Pommes Anna
ingredients as for Pommes Voisin,
omitting the Parmesan cheese.

Slice the peeled potatoes into rounds about $\frac{1}{16}$ inch thick (slicing on a mandolin is easiest).

Generously butter a 6-inch round cake pan and arrange a layer of potatoes in a circle over the base, neatly overlapping each slice. Drizzle with a little of the melted butter, sprinkle with some of the Parmesan, and season with salt and pepper. Continue layering, drizzling with butter, sprinkling with cheese, and seasoning, until all the potatoes have been used.

Drizzle the remaining butter over the top and bake in a preheated oven at 425°F for about 40 to 50 minutes or until very tender. Press down the potato slices 3 or 4 times during baking to form a solid cake.

Variations:

Pommes Voisin with Jerusalem Artichokes

Peel and slice the artichokes in the same way as the potatoes, dropping them into a bowl of water acidulated with the lemon juice to prevent discoloration. Drain and pat dry just before using. Alternate layers of artichokes with layers of potato and proceed as in the main recipe.

Pommes Anna

Follow the main recipe, omitting the Parmesan cheese.

potato noodles
with red cherry compote

These noodles are not long and thin as one might think, but rather little fried squares of potato and semolina, served either savory or sweet. This sweet cherry compote is based on an original German recipe.

Place the potatoes in a saucepan, cover with cold water, bring to a boil, then simmer for 25 to 30 minutes until tender. When cool enough to handle, peel and pass through a potato ricer or food mill into a clean saucepan.

Put the saucepan on the heat and gradually beat in the milk until smooth. Cook, beating continuously (do not allow to catch or burn) until the mixture starts to boil. Sprinkle in the semolina in a thin stream, beating all the time. Continue cooking until the mixture thickens. Remove from the heat and beat in the eggs.

Spread onto a lightly greased 9 x 13-inch jelly roll pan and smooth the surface. Let cool completely. Turn the mixture out onto a work surface and cut into 1-inch strips. Cut across again into small squares or diamonds.

To make the compote, combine the cherries in a saucepan with the 2 tablespoons sugar, orange zest, and juice. Stir well and bring to a boil. Reduce the heat, cover, and simmer for 5 to 10 minutes or until the cherries are tender. Remove from the heat and stir in the Kirsch. Set aside.

Combine the 6 tablespoons sugar and cinnamon in a pan, heat well and stir, then transfer to a large plate or tray. Melt the butter in a large skillet, add the potato squares, and cook until lightly golden on both sides. Drain well on paper towels then transfer them to the tray of cinnamon sugar. Toss well to coat, shaking off any excess.

Serve with sour cream and the warm compote, scattered with the toasted almonds.

1 lb. floury potatoes, unpeeled
2¾ cups milk
6 tablespoons fine semolina
2 large eggs, beaten
6 tablespoons superfine sugar
½ teaspoon ground cinnamon
6 tablespoons butter
Red Cherry Compote:
1 lb. sweet red cherries, stoned, or
frozen ones, thawed with juice retained
2 tablespoons superfine sugar
1 strip orange zest
juice of 1 orange
2 tablespoons Kirsch
sour cream, to serve
½ cup flaked almonds, toasted
Serves 4

kartoffelnudeln

An updated version of a traditional, old-fashioned bread. Potato and potato flour produce bread with a moist texture that keeps well and is very good toasted. Potato flour has no gluten, so whenever it is used alone in recipes, it is suitable for people on gluten-free diets.

honey potato bread
with saffron and poppyseed glaze

8 oz. floury potatoes, peeled

a large pinch of saffron strands

2¾ cups bread flour

1 teaspoon salt

1½ teaspoons active dry yeast

2 tablespoons liquid honey

6 tablespoons unsalted butter, melted

2 large egg yolks, beaten

¾ cup raisins

Poppyseed Glaze:

1 large egg white, beaten

1 tablespoon black poppyseeds

Makes 2 loaves

Add the potatoes to a saucepan of boiling water, reduce the heat, and simmer until tender. Drain, reserving 1 cup of the cooking water in a bowl, then steep the saffron strands in the water for about 30 minutes.

Press the drained potatoes through a potato ricer, food mill, or fine sieve into a large bowl. Add the reserved potato water and saffron and mix together well.

Sift the flour and salt into a large bowl and stir in the dry yeast. Add the potato mixture, honey, butter, egg yolks, and raisins and mix well to form a soft but firm dough.

Tip the dough onto a floured work surface and knead well for 10 minutes. Transfer to an oiled bowl or oiled plastic bag, cover the bowl or tie the bag, and leave in a warm place for about 1 to 1½ hours or until doubled in size.

Tip the dough onto a floured work surface, punch down, and knead well for a further 5 minutes. Cut in half and form into 2 round loaves. Place on 2 greased baking trays and score each loaf with a knife in a criss-cross pattern. Cover loosely and let rise again in a warm place for 45 minutes to 1 hour, until doubled in size.

Brush with egg white and sprinkle with poppyseeds. Bake in a preheated oven at 400°F for 40 minutes or until the bottom of the loaf sounds hollow when tapped. Cool on a wire rack and eat within 5 days, or freeze for up to 1 month.

Scottish cooks are famous throughout Britain for their baking skills, and scones (biscuits) are perhaps their finest achievement. Scottish scones are cooked with many different flavorings, but the Parmesan cheese and pancetta used in this recipe reflect the influence of the large Italian-Scottish community living "north of the border." Mashed potato is used to replace some of the flour, giving the biscuits a light, moist texture.

golden potato biscuits
with parmesan and pancetta

4 slices pancetta or bacon (about 2 oz.), cut into small pieces
1 to 1⅛ cups all-purpose flour
2 teaspoons baking powder
½ teaspoon salt
4 tablespoons unsalted butter, diced
½ cup cooked mashed potato
2 oz. Parmesan cheese, cut into tiny cubes
1 teaspoon dried oregano
about 2 tablespoons milk
1 egg yolk, beaten, to glaze
Makes 10

Heat a skillet without oil and dry-fry the pancetta or bacon for 5 to 6 minutes or until crispy. Remove with a slotted spoon and let cool on paper towels.

Sift the flour, baking powder, and salt together into a large bowl. Add the butter and rub in until the mixture resembles breadcrumbs. Mix in the potato, Parmesan, oregano, and cooked pancetta or bacon pieces. Add enough milk to form a soft but firm dough.

Tip out onto a lightly floured work surface, and knead briefly. Roll out the dough to ½ inch thick and, using a fluted cutter, stamp out 2½-inch rounds. Re-roll any trimmings and cut more rounds, to make about 10 in total.

Place the biscuits on a well-greased baking tray, brush the tops with the beaten egg, and bake in a preheated oven at 425°F for 10 to 15 minutes or until golden brown and well risen. Cool a little on a wire rack, then serve while still warm, spread with unsalted butter.

the middle east

The precise date of the potato's adoption in the cuisines of the Middle East cannot be pinpointed. However the **sophisticated spicing** typical of the dishes from this region is perfectly suited to the flavor-absorbing properties of the potato.

This recipe is based on a Persian potato omelet with fava beans added. Use frozen fava beans if you can't find young fresh ones—the fava is one of the few foods that is almost as good frozen as fresh. Frozen ones are also easier to pop out of their little grey coats, leaving the brilliant green bean behind. This dish is good as a starter or served with drinks.

kuku sibzamini

kuku sibzamini

8 oz. fava beans, podded if fresh, defrosted if frozen
1 lb. cooked potatoes, mashed
6 large eggs, beaten
1 teaspoon ground turmeric
6 scallions, chopped
2 tablespoons chopped fresh cilantro
1 tablespoon chopped fresh flat-leaf parsley
salt and freshly ground black pepper
2 tablespoons unsalted butter

Serves 6 to 8 as a starter

If using young fresh fava beans, blanch them in lightly salted boiling water for 5 to 6 minutes (longer for older ones), then drain, refresh in cold water, then drain again. Pop the fresh or frozen fava beans out of their skins and set them aside. (Discard the skins.)

Put the mashed potato in a large bowl, then stir in the beaten eggs and ground turmeric. Fold in the fava beans, scallions, and herbs, and season with salt and freshly ground black pepper.

Melt the butter over a moderate heat in a heavy-bottom non-stick skillet with a heatproof handle. Pour in the potato mixture. Reduce the heat to very low and cook without stirring for 15 to 20 minutes or until the eggs have set and the base is golden brown (check by lifting the edge with a spatula).

Place the pan under the broiler to brown the top of the omelet, then slide the omelet onto a large plate or tray and cut into small squares or wedges.

Serve hot or cold.

The potato is known as *batata* in Arabic. This salad from Saudi Arabia combines a traditional Middle Eastern ingredient, the chickpea, with the more recent arrival, the potato. As carbohydrates packed full of fiber, both are particularly good for absorbing the spicy, sophisticated flavors typical of Middle Eastern food.

sultan's salad

¼ cup dried chickpeas (garbanzos)

1 to 2 garlic cloves, chopped

2 oz. shelled walnuts, chopped

4 tablespoons chopped fresh flat-leaf parsley

2 tablespoons chopped fresh mint

4 tablespoons tahini paste

4 to 5 tablespoons freshly squeezed lemon juice

⅓ cup extra-virgin olive oil

about ⅓ cup water

a pinch of paprika

sea salt

1½ lb. unpeeled new or waxy potatoes

To Serve (optional):

2 tablespoons chopped walnuts

1 tablespoon toasted sesame seeds

sprigs of mint

Serves 4

Place the chickpeas in a bowl, cover with cold water, and let soak overnight. The next day, drain the chickpeas and rinse well. Place them in a saucepan of unsalted cold water, bring to a boil, reduce the heat, and simmer for 50 minutes to 1 hour or until tender. Drain well and reserve in a large bowl.

Combine the garlic, walnuts, and herbs in the bowl of a food processor or blender. Pulse until finely chopped. Add the tahini paste and 4 tablespoons of the lemon juice and whizz to mix. With the motor running, add the olive oil in a thin steady stream until amalgamated. Add enough water to make a thin dressing.

Pour the sauce into a bowl and season to taste with salt, paprika, and some extra lemon juice if needed.

Add the potatoes to a saucepan of lightly salted boiling water and simmer for 15 to 20 minutes or until tender. Drain well, then cut the potatoes in half and add to the bowl with the chickpeas. Add the dressing and toss the mixture well while still warm.

Serve warm or cold, sprinkled with the chopped walnuts, toasted sesame seeds, and sprigs of fresh mint.

I was taught this recipe by the mother of Marwan Badran, a London-based Iraqi friend. Iraqi Seville oranges are sweeter than most, so after much testing of this recipe, the Badrans, *mère et fils*, found that substituting oranges and lemons produces the right balance of sweetness and sharpness. It is a wonderful, yellow-orange stew, heavily scented with all the spices of the Middle East.

chicken potato stew
with "Seville" oranges

a large pinch of saffron strands

2 tablespoons olive oil

1 whole chicken, about 4 lb., cut into 8 pieces

2 tablespoons all-purpose flour

1 teaspoon salt, plus extra to taste

black seeds from 6 green cardamom pods, crushed

1 teaspoon whole cloves

1 teaspoon allspice berries

1 teaspoon whole black peppercorns

1 teaspoon whole pink peppercorns

2 cinnamon sticks, 3 inches each

juice of 2 large oranges

juice of 2 large lemons

1½ lb. floury potatoes, peeled and cut into 3-inch chunks

1 whole orange, sliced

1 whole lemon, sliced

2 tablespoons rosewater (optional)

Serves 4

Place the saffron strands in a small heatproof bowl and pour over boiling water to cover. Set aside to infuse.

Heat the olive oil in a large stockpot and sauté the chicken, 2 or 3 pieces at a time, until lightly golden all over. Remove the pieces to a tray. Drain off all but 1 tablespoon of the fat. Add the flour and cook for 1 to 2 minutes, then add the saffron and its infusing water. Stir well.

Add the chicken pieces to the pot, add the salt, spices, and the orange and lemon juices. Pour over enough water to cover (about 5 cups), and bring to a boil. Add the potato pieces and the orange and lemon slices.

Reduce the heat to low, cover with a lid, and simmer gently for 30 to 35 minutes or until tender, occasionally skimming off any fat that rises to the surface.

Taste and adjust the seasoning, then stir in rosewater, if using, to taste. Serve with rice.

mai-al-naringe

potato chap

This is an Iraqi version of the Lebanese *kibbeh,* which are usually made with bulgar wheat instead of potato. For *chap*, cooked potato is mashed and formed into a thin shell by hand and filled with spiced ground meat. Making *chap* requires a little skillful artistry and a good *chap* maker is highly admired for her deft finger work in creating perfect little ovals or globes with tiny pinched ends. *Chap* and *kibbeh* are a very common form of street food in the Middle East, equivalent to spring rolls or sausage rolls. They can be served as a snack, or for lunch squashed into pita bread with salad and creamy tahini sauce.

2 lb. floury potatoes, unpeeled, scrubbed well
1 tablespoon cornstarch
1 teaspoon salt
1 large egg, beaten
2 tablespoons fine dry breadcrumbs
Spicy Meat Filling:
2 tablespoons olive oil
1 large onion, finely chopped
½ cup pignoli nuts
1 lb. ground lamb or beef
1½ teaspoons mixed spice*
⅓ cup raisins
salt and freshly ground black pepper
4 tablespoons chopped fresh flat-leaf parsley
½ cup fine dry breadcrumbs
vegetable oil, for deep-frying
Makes 16

*Mixed spice is a traditional flavoring combination. In a spice grinder, grind 1 tablespoon each of ground coriander, ginger, cinnamon, and nutmeg, and 1 teaspoon each of allspice and cloves. Keep in an airtight container and use in cakes, breads, and meat dishes.

chap

1 Boil the potatoes in salted water for 15 to 20 minutes until tender (test after 15 minutes). Drain, peel, and pass through a food mill into a large bowl. Beat in the cornstarch, salt and egg. Knead and mix in the breadcrumbs.

2 To make the filling, heat the oil in a heavy-bottom pan, add the onion, and sauté for 5 to 6 minutes until softened and translucent. Add the pignoli nuts and cook for about 5 minutes until golden.

3 Add the meat, mixed spice, raisins, and seasonings to the pan and cook for about 10 to 15 minutes until brown and no liquid remains. Stir in the parsley, check the seasoning, drain in a sieve, and pat dry on kitchen paper.

4 Divide the potato mixture into 16 portions. Dip your hands in water and put one portion in your palm. Make an indentation with your thumb and pinch the sides while turning the ball in your palm to form a thin, even shell.

5 Put 1 tablespoon of the spiced meat mixture in the hole and smooth the sides of the pastry around the mixture.

6 Gradually pinch the opening closed and smooth it over, forming a flat oval and patting the surface until smooth. Patch any holes with a little extra potato mixture. Place on a tray and repeat with the remaining mixture.

7 Spread the breadcrumbs on a plate or tray and gently roll each oval *chap* in the breadcrumbs until evenly covered. Pat the breadcrumbs on gently so they stick well, then shake off any excess crumbs.

8 Fill a deep pan ⅓ full of oil and heat to 375°F or until a cube of bread browns in 30 seconds. Deep-fry the *chap* in batches until cooked and golden brown. Drain on paper towels and serve hot with pita bread and salad.

Some **New World** vegetables, formerly thought to have been introduced to the rest of the world **after 1492**, may have been taken to Africa **much earlier**, by Arab seafarers in the middle of the **first millenium**. Potatoes may have reached Africa at that time.

africa

moroccan couscous

Couscous is the national dish of Morocco, traditionally made in a *couscousière*—a large, double-layered pot. It is much more easily made these days thanks to the advent of easy-cook couscous. I learned how to make this dish from a Moroccan chef I worked with in Switzerland, who cooked this dish as a treat for the staff. Recent scholarship suggests that it may have been Arab seafarers from the Atlantic coast of Morocco who brought New World ingredients to North and West Africa during medieval times, when Arab art and scholarship reached its zenith, and Europe was still mired in the Dark Ages.

¾ cup dried chickpeas (garbanzos),
soaked overnight in cold water

1½ lb. lean lamb, shoulder or leg,
cut into 1½-inch pieces

2 onions, chopped

3 tablespoons olive oil

2 cinnamon sticks

½ teaspoon ground ginger

a large pinch of saffron strands

¼ teaspoon cayenne pepper
or chile powder

3 turnips, halved or quartered if large

1 lb. small new potatoes, halved

8 oz. pumpkin, peeled and cubed

13 oz. shelled fava beans,
defrosted if frozen

8 oz. ripe tomatoes,
peeled, seeded, and chopped

2¾ cups easy-cook couscous

½ cup raisins

6 tablespoons chopped
fresh cilantro leaves

salt and freshly ground black pepper

½ cup whole blanched almonds

3 tablespoons chopped
fresh flat-leaf parsley

¼ cup unsalted butter

Serves 4

Drain and rinse the chickpeas and place in the bottom of a two-part steamer or *couscousière* with the lamb and onions. Add 2 tablespoons of the oil, the cinnamon, ginger, saffron, and cayenne or chile powder to the pot (do not add salt at this point or it will make the chickpeas tough). Add about 3 cups cold water, or enough just to cover.

Bring to a boil, reduce the heat, cover, and simmer for 1 hour.

Add the turnips, potatoes, pumpkin, fava beans (if fresh), and the tomatoes, and continue cooking for another 20 minutes.

Meanwhile, place the couscous in a large bowl and stir in hot water following the package instructions. Leave for 15 to 20 minutes to allow the grains to swell, stirring occasionally with a fork to fluff up the grains.

Stir the fava beans (if frozen), raisins, and cilantro into the stew and season with salt and pepper if needed. Add the prepared couscous to the top compartment of the *couscousière*. If using a steamer which has large holes in the top compartment, line with a layer of cheesecloth before adding the couscous. Cover and cook for 20 to 30 minutes, fluffing up the grains occasionally with a fork.

Heat the remaining oil in a skillet, add the blanched almonds, and fry gently for 3 to 4 minutes or until golden brown. Stir the parsley into the stew, taste, and adjust the seasoning. Tip the couscous into a large bowl and stir in the butter until melted, fluffing up the grains. Spoon the stew over the couscous and scatter with the toasted almonds.

Peanuts and plantains are widely used by cooks all over Sub-Saharan Africa, especially in West Africa. Though the potato is not indigenous to Africa, it is now used almost as much as its fellow imports, cassava and sweet potatoes, and native tubers, such as yams and taro. Variations of this soup can be made with any of these root vegetables.

potato peanut soup
with deep-fried plantain strips

3 tablespoons peanut oil

1 large onion, chopped

¼ teaspoon dried, crushed red chiles

4 medium tomatoes, peeled and chopped

1 lb. floury potatoes, peeled and cut into 1-inch cubes

1 cup roasted, unsalted peanuts

5 cups chicken stock

sea salt, to season

To Serve:

1 plantain

vegetable oil, for deep-frying

⅓ cup raw unsalted peanuts

a pinch of ground ginger

3 scallions, finely chopped

Serves 4

Heat 2 tablespoons of the oil in a large saucepan, add the onion and crushed red chiles, and cook for 5 to 6 minutes or until the onion is softened and translucent but not colored. Add the tomatoes, potatoes, peanuts, and stock, season with salt and cook for 15 to 20 minutes or until the potato is very tender. Remove from the heat and purée in a blender or food processor, in batches if necessary, then strain through a sieve into a clean pan. To peel the plantain, make a slit with a small knife from the stalk down to the end, run your thumb under the skin, and peel it back. With a potato peeler, slice the plantain very thinly lengthwise, then cut each slice into ¼-inch strips. Fill a deep pan ⅓ full of vegetable oil and heat to 375°F, or until a cube of bread browns in 30 seconds. Deep-fry the plantain strips, a few at a time, until crisp and golden, then drain on paper towels.

Heat the remaining peanut oil in a skillet over low heat. Add the peanuts and sauté for 1 to 2 minutes until just beginning to brown, then add a pinch of ground ginger and continue to cook until the peanuts are golden brown all over. Remove from the heat and scoop onto paper towels to drain.

Reheat the soup, check the seasoning, and serve garnished with the plantain, peanuts, and chopped scallion.

The Portuguese introduced New World ingredients to Asia—and now it is impossible to think of **Southeast Asian** food without chiles, or **Indian** cooking without potatoes (*aloo*)—so perfect with their **complex spice mixtures**.

asia

potato pakoras

with spicy tomato chutney

Pakoras are deep-fried Indian fritters made from potatoes or other vegetables dipped in chickpea (gram) flour batter. They are usually served with tea for lunch (tiffin), or as snacks or street food at almost any time of the day. Nigella (*kalonji*) are black teardrop-shaped seeds with a peppery, lemon flavor and are often incorrectly sold as black onion seeds. Dried pomegranate seeds (*anardhana*) are used predominantly in North Indian cooking. They have a pleasant sweet-sour flavor and should be slightly sticky to the touch. Both spices are sold in Asian grocers and specialist delicatessens.

Tomato Chutney:

2 lb. ripe tomatoes, peeled and chopped

1 large onion, chopped

2 to 3 garlic cloves, crushed

1-inch piece fresh gingerroot, peeled and finely chopped

⅔ cup white wine vinegar

1 teaspoon salt

¼ teaspoon crushed dried red chiles

¼ teaspoon ground cloves

¼ teaspoon ground cardamon

¼ teaspoon ground cinnamon

1 cup brown sugar

Pakoras:

1⅔ cups gram (chickpea) flour

1 tablespoon dried pomegranate seeds, ground

1 tablespoon nigella seeds

1 fresh green chile, seeded and finely chopped

½ teaspoon ground turmeric

1 teaspoon ground cumin

1 teaspoon salt

¾ to 1 cup water

1 lb. potatoes, peeled and cut into ¼-inch slices

vegetable oil, for deep-frying

Serves 6 as a snack

To make the chutney, combine the tomatoes, onion, garlic, and ginger in a large heavy-bottom saucepan, stir to mix, and cook over a medium heat for about 30 minutes until reduced to a thick pulp.

Reduce the heat to low and stir in the remaining ingredients. Cook, stirring occasionally (do not allow it to catch on the bottom), for about 30 to 40 minutes until fairly thick. Pour into a sterilized jar while still hot.

To make the pakoras, combine all the dry ingredients in a large bowl, then gradually mix in the water to make a fairly thick batter. Fill a deep pan ⅓ full with vegetable oil and heat to 375°F, or until a cube of bread browns in 30 seconds. Dip the potato slices in the batter, add to the oil in batches, and fry until golden brown all over, about 5 to 8 minutes. Drain on paper towels.

Serve hot with the tomato chutney or either of the variations below.

Variations:

Eggplant and Cilantro Raita

Put a whole eggplant under a very hot broiler or in a hot oven and cook, turning occasionally, until charred and very soft. Let cool, slit down the middle, and squeeze to remove any bitter juices. With a spoon, scoop the flesh into a bowl and mash well with a fork. Let cool completely. Add 1¼ cups plain yogurt, 3 tablespoons chopped fresh cilantro, season to taste with salt and pepper, and serve sprinkled with garam masala (from Asian food stores).

Fresh Green Mint and Cilantro Chutney

Put 6 tablespoons each of chopped fresh mint and fresh cilantro leaves in a small food processor or spice grinder. Add 4 chopped green chiles (seeded if preferred), 2 teaspoons sugar, 2 teaspoons garam masala (see above), ½ teaspoon salt, and 2 tablespoons fresh lemon juice. Add 1 or 2 tablespoons cold water if needed and process until smooth. Scrape into a serving bowl, taste, and add extra lemon juice if required.

roti

India has dozens of different kinds of bread—plain, flavored with spices as here, or with spicy fillings. They are served with curry or dhaal, but these roti are made smaller to eat as a snack. Carry through the potato theme and serve roti with vodka-based drinks—vodka is sometimes made from potatoes, as well as from grains.

mini potato roti
with coconut and mint chutney

Coconut and Mint Chutney:
1½ **cups grated fresh coconut or ⅔ cup**
unsweetened desiccated coconut
1 cup plain yogurt
1 green chile, seeded and chopped
2 tablespoons chopped fresh mint
½ **teaspoon salt**
½ **teaspoon sugar**
Roti:
1½ **lb. large floury potatoes, peeled**
2 fresh green chiles
½ **teaspoon crushed dried red chiles**
1 small onion, finely chopped
1 teaspoon salt
1 teaspoon ground cumin
1 teaspoon ground turmeric
2 tablespoons chopped
fresh cilantro leaves
2 tablespoons unsalted butter, melted
1 cup all-purpose flour
vegetable oil, for frying
Makes 64

If using desiccated coconut to make the chutney, place in a bowl and cover with warm water. Let soak for about 20 minutes, then strain through a sieve, pressing the coconut against the sides of the sieve to squeeze out any excess moisture. Combine all the chutney ingredients in a bowl, mix well, and set aside.

Cook the potatoes in boiling salted water, drain, and mash well. Seed and finely chop the green chiles. Add to the potatoes and stir in all the remaining ingredients, except the flour. Gradually mix in the flour until you have a soft dough. Divide the dough into equal-sized pieces. Taking one piece at a time, roll out on a floured board to a 3-inch circle. Continue with the remaining pieces. Brush a heavy-based skillet with oil and, when hot, cook the roti 2 or 3 at a time for 1 to 2 minutes on each side until lightly browned.

Serve with the coconut and mint chutney.

samosas

vegetable samosas
with potato and cauliflower

These crisp little triangular vegetable parcels are usually eaten as street food snacks and are found throughout India. Portuguese seafarers introduced New World ingredients such as chiles, bell peppers, corn, and potatoes to India. The Portuguese were the earliest European traders in the area—a major mercantile power from Renaissance times, and their influence persisted until they were forcibly ejected from the west-coast colony of Goa in the 1960s, almost twenty years after India gained independence in 1947.

Pastry:

2 cups all-purpose flour

½ teaspoon salt

4 tablespoons vegetable oil

8 tablespoons water

Cauliflower Potato Filling:

1 lb. floury potatoes, unpeeled and scrubbed

8 oz. small cauliflower florets

2 tablespoons vegetable oil

1 teaspoon black mustard seeds

1 onion, finely chopped

1 tablespoon finely grated fresh gingerroot

1 or 2 green chiles, seeded and very finely chopped

1 teaspoon ground coriander

½ teaspoon ground turmeric

1 teaspoon garam masala

½ teaspoon cayenne pepper

½ teaspoon salt

1 to 2 tablespoons lemon juice

3 tablespoons chopped fresh cilantro leaves

vegetable oil, for deep-frying

Makes 18

1 To make the pastry, sift the flour and salt into a bowl, then rub in the oil. Gradually add water to make a firm dough, then tip onto a lightly floured surface. Knead 5 minutes until smooth, cover, and let rest 30 minutes to 1 hour.

2 Boil the potatoes in salted water for 15 to 20 minutes until just tender. Drain, peel, and cut into ½-inch dice. Blanch the cauliflower briefly in boiling salted water, drain, refresh in plenty of cold water and drain again well.

3 Heat the oil in a pan, sauté the mustard seeds until they pop, add the onions, ginger, and chile and cook for 5 to 6 minutes. Add spices and salt and cook 1 to 2 minutes. Add the potatoes, cauliflower, and 1 tablespoon lemon juice.

5 Cut a circle in half and brush the edges with water. Add 1 tablespoon filling and fold the pastry to form a cone. Press the straight edges to seal. Fold the rounded edges together and crimp to seal. Repeat with the remaining circles.

4 Cook for 2 to 3 minutes. Remove from the heat, add chopped cilantro, salt, and lemon juice to taste. Let cool. Divide the pastry into 9 balls. Working with one at a time and keeping the others covered, roll each into a 7-inch circle.

6 Fill a wide, deep pan ⅓ full of oil and heat to 375°F or until a cube of bread browns in 30 seconds. Cook 2 to 3 samosas at a time for 4 to 5 minutes, turning once, until golden. Drain on paper towels and serve with chutney.

Popiah—delicious fillings wrapped in spring roll wrappers, ricepaper, or pancakes —are a popular snack food in Malaysia. Use this mixture of two flours to make the pancakes, or use all-purpose flour only.

popiah
Malaysian popiah

1 cup all-purpose flour and ½ cup rice flour
½ teaspoon salt
2 large eggs, beaten
about 1¾ cups water
2 tablespoons vegetable oil,
plus extra for frying
Shrimp and Ginger Filling:
15 uncooked medium shrimp, peeled
2 tablespoons vegetable oil
1 teaspoon finely grated gingerroot
2 garlic cloves, very thinly sliced
1 waxy potato (about 7 oz.),
peeled, grated, and squeezed dry
1 medium carrot, grated
4 oz. daikon (white radish) grated
2½ tablespoons sweet yellow bean paste
6 scallions, trimmed and finely shredded
½ small cucumber, grated
4 cups beansprouts
2 oz. firm bean curd (tofu), crumbled
salt and freshly ground black pepper
6 red chiles, seeded and crushed to a paste
12 crisp lettuce leaves
1 small bunch fresh cilantro
soy sauce and sliced red chile, to serve
Makes 12

To make the pancakes, sift the flour/s and salt into a bowl. Make a well in the center, add the eggs, and beat, adding enough water to make a thin batter. Strain through a sieve and stir in the oil. Let rest for 30 minutes before using.

To make the filling, devein and chop the shrimp. Heat the oil in a skillet, add the ginger and garlic, and sauté for 1 to 2 minutes until softened and golden. Add the shrimp and fry for 1 minute. Add the grated potato, carrot, and daikon and stir-fry for 1 to 2 minutes until just tender but still firm. Add the yellow bean paste and stir-fry for 1 minute. Remove from the heat and stir in the scallion, cucumber, beansprouts, and beancurd. Season to taste with salt and pepper and let cool.

Heat a non-stick crêpe pan or skillet and add a little oil. Tip out any excess oil, then pour in a ladle of the batter—enough to make a thin pancake. Swirl around to cover the base. Cook for 1 to 2 minutes until lightly browned, turn it over, and cook the other side briefly. Repeat with the remaining batter to make 12 pancakes.

To assemble the *popiah*, spread each pancake with some crushed chile, line with a lettuce leaf, and top with some of the cooked filling. Add a few cilantro leaves, roll up tightly, leaving the ends open, and cut into 2 or 3 slices. Alternatively, serve the filling ingredients separately for the guests to assemble. Serve with a dip of soy sauce sprinkled with sliced red chile.

kaeng kai
thai chicken curry
with potatoes and coconut milk

A delicious, very simple curry with all the flavors of Thailand. Fish sauce (*nam pla*) and delicious Thai curry pastes are available in Southeast Asian stores. The curry pastes can be bought, ready-made, in either red, green, orange mussaman (Muslim), or paenang. The red paste is much more fiery than the green, while the mussaman paste is quite mild. Starchy foods like potatoes and rice have a particular affinity for the assertive spicy flavorings found in Southeast Asia.

2 tablespoons vegetable oil
1 ½ lb. boneless chicken (breasts or thighs), cut into large chunks
2 to 3 tablespoons red or green Thai curry paste
2¾ cups canned coconut milk
2½ tablespoons Thai fish sauce (*nam pla*)
2 tablespoons brown sugar
1 lb. new potatoes, unpeeled, scrubbed, and cut in half
½ teaspoon salt
1 to 2 tablespoons lime juice
To Serve:
⅓ cup unsalted roasted peanuts
3 scallions, cut into fine shreds and put in a bowl of ice water
Thai basil or cilantro, coarsely chopped
2 kaffir lime leaves, finely sliced (optional)
Serves 4

1 Heat the vegetable oil in a large wok or skillet, add the chicken pieces, in batches if necessary, and sauté them briefly on all sides to seal. Remove the chicken pieces to a bowl.

2 Add the curry paste to the pan and stir-fry for about 30 seconds to release the aromas of the chiles and spices.

3 Add the coconut milk, fish sauce, and sugar to the pan and stir well to combine. Return the sautéed chicken pieces to the pan, together with any juices that have accumulated in the bowl.

4 Bring the mixture to a boil, then add the potato halves and salt, and reduce the heat. Cover the pan and simmer for about 15 to 20 minutes until the chicken is cooked and the potatoes are tender.

5 Stir in the lime juice to taste and more salt if needed. Serve sprinkled with the peanuts, scallion strips, basil or cilantro, and the kaffir lime strips, if using. Steamed jasmine rice is a suitable accompaniment.

The potato, known as *aloo* in several Indian languages, is an important ingredient for the large vegetarian Hindu population. It revolutionized nutrition in mountain areas, such as the Khumbu on the slopes of Mt. Everest, where the yield is more reliable than the grain crops it replaced.

Indian dry potato curry
in eggplant shells with yogurt

2 large eggplants

1½ lb. waxy potatoes, peeled and cut into ½-inch cubes

6 to 8 tablespoons vegetable oil

1 tablespoon cumin seeds

1 teaspoon black mustard seeds

1 teaspoon sesame seeds

1 onion, finely chopped

1 to 2 garlic cloves, crushed

1 teaspoon grated fresh gingerroot

1 fresh green chile, seeded and finely chopped

½ teaspoon ground turmeric

1 teaspoon ground coriander

½ teaspoon salt, plus extra for sprinkling

1 to 2 tablespoons lemon or lime juice

To Serve:

4 tablespoons plain yogurt

garam masala, for sprinkling

2 tablespoons chopped fresh cilantro leaves

Serves 4

Cut the eggplants in half lengthwise and, using a spoon, scoop out the flesh, leaving a ¼-inch shell. Cut the flesh into ½-inch dice. Sprinkle the inside of the eggplant shells with salt and put in a colander, cut side down. Spread the eggplant cubes on a plate or tray or in a colander and sprinkle with more salt. Leave for about 30 minutes, then rinse well and pat dry with paper towels.

Bring a saucepan of lightly salted water to a boil, add the potato cubes, and cook for 5 minutes. Drain well and let cool. Place the eggplant shells, cut side up, on a baking tray, brush with 2 tablespoons of the oil, and bake in a preheated oven at 375°F for 10 to 15 minutes until softened.

Remove from the oven and turn the eggplant shells upside down on a plate to drain off any excess oil.

Heat another 2 tablespoons of the oil in a large skillet, add the cumin, mustard, and sesame seeds and when they start to pop add the onion, garlic, ginger, and chile. Stir-fry for about 2 to 3 minutes then add the eggplant cubes. Cook, stirring occasionally, for 4 to 5 minutes or until they are just cooked, adding more oil as needed.

Stir in the turmeric, ground coriander, and salt, then add the potatoes and stir-fry for 5 to 6 minutes until the potatoes are golden. Remove from the heat and stir in the lemon or lime juice. Taste and adjust the seasoning.

Put the eggplants back on the baking tray, cut side up. Divide the potato mixture evenly between them and return to the oven for 10 minutes to heat through.

Serve with the yogurt and sprinkle with a little garam masala (from Asian food stores) and the chopped fresh cilantro.

Dhaal baht (rice and lentils) is a staple meal for millions of Indians and Nepalis. In this recipe, potatoes (*aloo*) are added to that traditional duo, and they are particularly desirable for their ability to absorb the wonderful flavors of Indian spices.

dhaal aloo

Indian potato curry
with toor dhaal (yellow lentils)

Wash the lentils well in several changes of water. Heat the oil in a large saucepan over a low heat. Add the mustard and fenugreek seeds. When they begin to pop, stir in the ginger and garlic and sauté for 30 seconds. Add the cayenne pepper, ground coriander, and turmeric and stir-fry for a further 30 seconds.

Add the tomatoes and lentils to the pan, cover with 2¾ cups water, add the salt, and bring to a boil. Reduce the heat, cover, and simmer for 20 to 30 minutes or until the lentils are just soft. Add the potatoes and simmer over a low heat for 10 to 15 minutes or until tender. Taste and adjust the seasoning. Sprinkle with chopped cilantro and garam masala (from Asian food stores), add sprigs of fresh cilantro, and serve. Basmati rice and naan bread make suitable accompaniments.

1¼ cups yellow lentils

3 tablespoons oil

½ teaspoon mustard seeds

½ teaspoon fenugreek seeds

1 teaspoon grated fresh gingerroot

1 teaspoon crushed garlic

1 teaspoon cayenne pepper

1½ teaspoons ground coriander

½ teaspoon ground turmeric

4 tomatoes, peeled and chopped

1 teaspoon salt

1½ lb. floury potatoes, peeled and diced

2 tablespoons chopped fresh cilantro, plus extra sprigs, to serve

½ teaspoon garam masala, to serve

Serves 4

Australia and New Zealand have many unique varieties of potatoes, adapted to their wide range of climates. Chefs Down Under are brilliantly innovative, blending **European and Asian** traditions, and are keen to work with **new and unusual** varieties of all kinds of foods.

australia
and new zealand

thai-style fish fingers

with frothy lime and lemongrass hollandaise

This dish is a perfect example of the eclectic influences found in Australian cooking. Australia's first settlers were British, followed by the Chinese, who came during the nineteenth-century gold rushes, then by post-war immigrants from central and southern Europe. The most recent immigrants are from the Middle East and all over Southeast Asia. The result is an exciting culinary mix, generally known as Pacific Rim or fusion food. This recipe is a Southeast Asian twist on an old-fashioned English food, the hilariously named "fish finger," with a classic French hollandaise plus Asian flavorings.

2 tablespoons unsalted butter

6 scallions, finely chopped

1 garlic clove, crushed

1-inch piece of fresh gingerroot, peeled and finely grated

1 red chile, seeded and finely chopped

7 oz. fresh white crabmeat

2 tablespoons chopped fresh cilantro

1 teaspoon Thai fish sauce (nam pla)

8 oz. floury potatoes, cooked and mashed

1 large egg, separated

salt and freshly ground black pepper

½ cup fresh breadcrumbs

⅓ cup unsweetened desiccated coconut

butter or sunflower oil, for cooking

Lime and Lemongrass Hollandaise:

1⅔ cups unsalted butter

3 stalks lemongrass, chopped

3 tablespoons freshly squeezed lime juice

finely grated zest of 1 lime (preferably kaffir lime)

1 teaspoon white peppercorns, lightly crushed

1 shallot, finely chopped

3 large eggs, separated

Serves 4

To start the hollandaise, gently heat the butter and lemongrass in a small saucepan until the butter is melted. Remove from the heat, cover, and set aside for 2 to 3 hours. (Keep it in a warm place so it doesn't solidify.)

To make the fish fingers, melt the 2 tablespoons butter in a pan, add the scallions, garlic, ginger, and chile, cook gently for 5 minutes until softened, then transfer to a bowl and stir in the crab, cilantro, and fish sauce. Add the potato and beaten egg yolk and mix well to combine. Season to taste with salt and freshly ground black pepper.

Divide the mixture into 12 pieces and form each into a 1 x 4-inch rectangle. Beat the egg white lightly with a fork, mix the breadcrumbs and coconut together, and place in separate shallow bowls. Coat each fish finger in the egg white and then coat evenly in the crumb mixture. Set aside on a tray until ready to cook.

Heat a little butter or oil in a skillet and cook the fish fingers in batches, for 3 to 4 minutes or until golden brown all over, then transfer to a baking tray and keep them warm while you complete the hollandaise.

Put 2 tablespoons of the lime juice, 2 tablespoons water, lime zest, peppercorns, and shallot in a small pan and boil until reduced to 1 tablespoon. While still warm, strain through a fine sieve into a bowl set over a pan of hot but not boiling water.

Add the egg yolks and beat well with a whisk. Continue beating and add the butter in a thin steady stream (leaving the sediment and lemongrass pieces in the bottom of the pan) until all the butter has been added and the hollandaise is thick and glossy. If it is very thick, beat in a spoonful of hot water. Season to taste with salt, pepper, and more lime juice if needed and remove from the heat.

In a separate bowl, beat the egg whites until stiff but not dry. Stir one-third of the egg white into the hollandaise, then carefully fold in the rest.

Serve immediately with the fish fingers.

Many Australian immigrants still follow their family cooking traditions. Maria, the mother of my great friend Pina, left Calabria in Southern Italy for Melbourne 35 years ago. She still dries her own tomatoes, setting them on wicker trays covered with net curtains on the garage roof. This recipe is a fine example of how the ingredients of one culture are absorbed into another.

potato mussel soup
with Italian sun-dried tomatoes

a pinch of saffron strands
½ cup boiling water
¾ cup dry white wine
2 lb. mussels, scrubbed, debearded, broken or open ones discarded
about 4 cups fish or chicken stock
2 tablespoons olive oil
I onion, sliced
I or 2 garlic cloves, crushed
I-inch piece fresh gingerroot, peeled and finely grated
I lb. potatoes, cut into I-inch cubes
8 oz. tomatoes, peeled and chopped
8 to10 sun-dried tomatoes, finely chopped
grated zest and juice of I orange
I sprig thyme
salt and freshly ground black pepper
chopped fresh flat-leaf parsley, to serve

Serves 4

Put the saffron in a small heatproof bowl, pour in the boiling water, and set aside to infuse. Pour the white wine into a pot large enough to accommodate all the mussels. Bring to a boil, add the mussels, cover with a tight-fitting lid, and cook, shaking the pan frequently, for 2 to 3 minutes until the mussels have opened. Tip the mussels into a colander set over a bowl to collect the juice and discard any mussels that have not opened. Remove two-thirds of the mussels from their shells, discard the empty shells, and set all the mussels aside. Strain the mussel liquid through a cheesecloth-lined sieve or coffee filter paper into a measuring cup. Measure the liquid and add fish or chicken stock or water to make 4 cups. Set aside.

Heat the olive oil in a large saucepan, add the onion, garlic, and ginger and cook for 5 to 10 minutes until the onion is softened and translucent. Add the potatoes, tomatoes, sun-dried tomatoes, and orange zest and cook for 1 to 2 minutes more. Add the reserved stock, the thyme, and the saffron in its soaking liquid, and bring to a boil. Reduce the heat and simmer for about 15 minutes until the potatoes are tender.

Add the orange juice and all the mussels. Season to taste with salt and pepper. Serve sprinkled with the chopped parsley.

pasta and potatoes
with macadamia pesto

This unusual—and beautiful—combination of pasta and potatoes comes from an Italian-Australian friend whose family came from Genoa. Though not traditional, it is characteristic of the exciting fusion food found in Australia. I have dressed it with a wonderfully oily pesto of macadamia nuts. Macadamias are native to tropical Australia, where they are known as "Queensland nuts." They have a wonderful creamy texture, perfect for making sauces.

To make the pesto, put the basil, macadamia nuts, and garlic in a blender or food processor and process until finely chopped. With the motor running, gradually add the oil in a thin stream until amalgamated. Scrape into a bowl, stir in the Parmesan, and season to taste with salt and pepper.

Bring a saucepan of lightly salted water to a boil, add the potatoes, and cook for 10 to 15 minutes, or until just tender. Drain and cool slightly, then peel and cut into ¼-inch slices. Cook the pasta in a large pot of boiling salted water according to the package instructions. Drain in a colander but leave 2 to 3 tablespoons of the cooking water in the bottom of the pot. (A small amount of cooking water will help the sauce to amalgamate and cling to the pasta.)

Return the pasta to the pot, add the potato slices and half of the pesto, and mix well. (Refrigerate the remaining pesto to use in another dish, such as the pesto mash on page 9.) Taste and adjust the seasoning and serve immediately with extra Parmesan cheese if desired.

1 lb. new or salad potatoes
1 lb. tagliatelle
Macadamia Pesto:
2 oz. fresh basil leaves
3 oz. unsalted macadamia nuts, coarsely chopped
2 garlic cloves, chopped
¾ cup extra-virgin olive oil
2 oz. Parmesan cheese, finely grated, plus extra to serve (optional)
salt and freshly ground black pepper
Serves 4

An extravagant dish of potatoes simmered gently in olive oil to melting tenderness. The oil can also be flavored with garlic cloves or rosemary sprigs. This recipe is good with baked or barbecued fish— Australians are passionate about fish, and salmon is now farmed in the chilly southern waters off the island state of Tasmania.

confit of potatoes
with pan-roasted salmon

1 red bell pepper

1 yellow bell pepper

3 tomatoes, peeled, seeded, and chopped

1 tablespoon chopped fresh chives

salt and freshly ground black pepper

4 cups good-quality extra-virgin olive oil*

1½ lb. medium waxy potatoes, peeled and cut into even ¼-inch slices

4 salmon fillets, 7 to 8 oz. each, seasoned on both sides

Serves 4

*Though this quantity of oil may seem extravagant, it can be strained after cooking and re-used.

Broil the whole bell peppers on a baking tray under a preheated broiler for 15 to 20 minutes, turning occasionally, until charred and blistered all over. Put the peppers in a plastic bag, tie the top, and let cool (the steam makes them easy to peel). When cool, peel and core the bell peppers, cut the flesh into small dice, and combine in a bowl with the tomatoes, chives, salt, and pepper. Set aside.

Pour the oil into a saucepan, add the potatoes, and bring to a very slow boil. When tiny bubbles rise to the surface, reduce the heat to very low and cook for 10 minutes. Test with the tip of a knife—the potatoes are cooked when they are still slightly firm in the center. (This is a crucial stage: the potatoes continue to cook when removed from the heat, and if over-cooked they will be an oily mush.) Remove from the heat and keep them warm in the oil.

Heat 1 tablespoon of the oil in a large ovenproof skillet over moderate heat. Place the fish in the pan, skin side down, and cook for 2 to 3 minutes until the skin is crispy and golden. Turn the pieces over and bake in a preheated oven at 400°F for 5 to 6 minutes or until just cooked.

Carefully remove the potato from the oil with a slotted metal spoon, drain, then divide between 4 plates. Place a salmon fillet on top, surround with the peppers and tomatoes, then serve.

straw potato pancakes
with barbecued duck breast

The use of pomegranates in this dish reflects the contribution to Australia's multi-cultural cuisine of immigrants from the Middle East, especially from Lebanon and Syria. Pomegranates are an important ingredient in Islamic cuisine, from Persia to Moghul India, the countries of Asia Minor, and across North Africa. Their brilliant color and sweet-sour flavor are an excellent complement to the richness of duck.

The crispy straw pancakes make a crunchy accompaniment to other meats, and like many potato dishes they sop up juices and gravies very well.

3 pomegranates, halved
rind of 1 preserved lemon, chopped
1 garlic clove, crushed
1-inch piece of fresh gingerroot, peeled and finely grated
4 small duck breasts
1 lb. waxy potatoes
salt and freshly ground pepper
about 2 tablespoons clarified butter
1 tablespoon hazelnut oil
2 tablespoons honey
a few salad leaves
⅓ cup roasted hazelnuts, chopped
Serves 4

1 Scoop out the pomegranate seeds, discarding the white pith. Reserve 3 tablespoons of seeds, cover, and chill. To make the marinade, put the remaining seeds in a blender and process briefly to release the juice.

2 Strain through a fine sieve into a flat non-metallic dish. Stir in the lemon rind, garlic, and ginger. Score the skin of the duck 3 or 4 times and put in the marinade. Turn to coat, cover, and chill for 12 to 24 hours, turning

3 With a mandolin or knife, cut the potatoes into thin julienne strips and place in cold water. Drain and rinse the potatoes 2 or 3 times to remove the starch. Drain, then dry well on a clean cloth. Place in a bowl and season.

4 Heat the butter and oil in a large pan. Add spoonfuls of the potato to make 4 little cakes. Press down slightly and cook for 8 to 10 minutes, turn over, and cook for 5 to 6 minutes more. Lift out of the pan and keep them warm.

5 Lift the duck from the marinade, pat dry, and place on a preheated broiler pan or barbecue. Broil, skin side down, for 5 minutes, then turn and broil 5 minutes longer until tender, but still pink. Set aside for 5 minutes. Slice thin.

6 Bring the marinade and honey to a boil in a small pan and reduce until thickened. Season to taste. To serve, place a pancake on each plate, top with duck and pomegranate seeds, then add sauce, salad leaves, and chopped nuts.

Here is an extravagant Australian version of the traditional British comfort food, "bangers and mash" (sausages and mashed potatoes). The poaching sauce for the sausages makes use of the great sparkling wines produced in Australia.

bangers and mash
champagne sausages with chestnut potato purée

Chestnut Potato Purée:

13 oz. fresh chestnuts (cut a slash in the pointed end of each one), or 8 oz. vacuum-packed chestnuts

1 small bulb fresh fennel, halved lengthwise, cored, and roughly chopped

½ cup milk

½ cup heavy cream

salt and freshly ground black pepper

2 lb. floury potatoes, unpeeled but well scrubbed

6 tablespoons unsalted butter

Champagne Sausages:

2 ripe pears

juice of 1 lemon

2 tablespoons unsalted butter

8 good-quality sausages, such as Italian-style

2 tablespoons brown sugar

1¾ cups champagne or good sparkling wine

Serves 4

If using fresh chestnuts to make the purée, place them in a saucepan, cover with cold water, bring to a boil, and simmer for 2 minutes. Remove the pan from the heat. Using a slotted spoon, remove one chestnut at a time and, using a small, sharp knife, remove the outer and inner skins. If the skins are difficult to peel, return the pan to the heat, return to a boil, and simmer for 2 minutes longer. Place the chestnuts in a small saucepan with the fennel, milk, and cream, bring to just below boiling, reduce the heat, and simmer gently for 30 to 40 minutes if using fresh chestnuts (15 to 20 minutes if using vacuum-packed), or until tender. Strain and reserve the liquid. Purée the chestnuts and fennel in a food processor until smooth, spoon into a bowl, season to taste, and set aside. In a deep pot, cover the potatoes with cold water, bring to a boil, and simmer for about 15 to 20 minutes until tender. Drain, peel, and press through a food mill, potato ricer, or sieve, then add the chestnut mixture and mix well.

Peel the pears, cut in half lengthwise, and scoop out the core. Cut each half into 6 slices, dropping into a bowl of water acidulated with the lemon juice. Drain well and pat dry on paper towels. Melt 1 tablespoon of the butter in a skillet, add the pear slices, and cook for about 4 to 5 minutes or until lightly golden. Remove with a slotted spoon and set aside. Add the remaining tablespoon of butter to the pan, add the sausages, and cook for 10 minutes until lightly golden. Add the sugar and wine, raise the heat to high, and boil for 2 to 3 minutes or until reduced by half. Add the sliced pears and heat through.

Put the chestnut-potato purée in a pan, stir in the 6 tablespoons butter and the reserved milk and cream mixture, and reheat, stirring to prevent sticking. Season to taste. Serve the sausages on top of the purée, then add the pears and sauce.

Tamarillos, or tree tomatoes, are a sub-tropical fruit, slightly soft when ripe, which can be eaten whole except for the skin. They are common in New Zealand gardens, and are often found in bigger supermarkets in other parts of the world. If unavailable, substitute plums, or even apricots.

potato-crust lamb
with poached tamarillos

1½ lb. waxy potatoes, peeled
1 garlic clove, crushed
2 tablespoons chopped fresh chives
2 tablespoons chopped fresh parsley
1 tablespoon fresh thyme leaves, removed from stalk
2 large egg yolks, beaten
salt and freshly ground black pepper
12 lamb cutlets, very well trimmed, with all fat removed and the bone scraped clean
3 tablespoons olive oil
sprigs of thyme, to serve
Poached Tamarillos:
6 tamarillos
⅔ cup port or red wine
⅔ cup lamb or chicken stock
3 tablespoons honey
2-inch cinnamon stick
½ teaspoon crushed coriander seeds
1 piece orange zest
Serves 4

Grate the potatoes finely and do not rinse. Wrap in a clean cloth and squeeze to extract any excess liquid. Put the grated potato in a bowl and add the garlic, herbs, and egg yolks. Season with salt and pepper and mix well. Divide into 12 and wrap each lamb cutlet completely with the mixture.

To prepare the tamarillos, use a sharp knife to cut a small cross at the pointed end of each one. Bring a saucepan of water to a boil, drop in the tamarillos, and blanch for 30 seconds. Lift out with a slotted spoon and plunge into cold water. To make the sauce, carefully peel all the tamarillos, and finely chop 2 of them.

Combine the port or red wine, stock, honey, cinnamon, crushed coriander seeds, orange zest, and the chopped tamarillo in a shallow pan. Bring to a boil, then reduce the heat, add the whole tamarillos, and simmer for 3 to 4 minutes. Lift the fruit out of the sauce and set aside. Increase the heat and boil rapidly for about 2 to 3 minutes or until well reduced.

Heat the oil over moderate heat in 2 large heavy-bottom skillets. Add the lamb cutlets and cook for 3 to 4 minutes on each side or until the potato is tender and crispy and the lamb is still pink. Slice the tamarillos, but leave them attached at the stalk, then place back into the sauce and reheat gently.

To serve, place 3 cutlets and 1 whole tamarillo on each plate. Drizzle over a little sauce and sprinkle with sprigs of thyme.

planning potato menus

Soups

Gingered seafood chowder with red roe cream and poppyseed crackers 18

Potage parmentier with parsley oil and croûtons 44

Potato mussel soup with Italian sun-dried tomatoes 128

Potato peanut soup with deep-fried plantain strips 102

Salads and Snacks

Blue potato salad 17

Empanaditas 24

Malaysian popiah 115

Mini potato roti with coconut and mint chutney 108

Potato chap 94

Potato pakoras with spicy tomato chutney 106

Roasted warm potato salad 17

Sultan's salad 91

Vegetable samosas with potato and cauliflower 110

Fish and Seafood

Confit of potatoes with pan-roasted salmon 133

Crispy potato tostadas with salmon and scallop seviche 16

Fish and chips: tuna strips with potato ribbons 42

Portuguese fish fritters with Greek skorthalia 68

Potato pancakes with mackerel gravad lax 47

Thai-style fish fingers with frothy lime and lemongrass hollandaise 126

Poultry

Chicken pot pie with porcini mushrooms and potato pastry 34

Chicken potato stew with "Seville" oranges 92

Potato turnovers with chicken livers 66

Straw potato pancakes with barbecued duck breasts 134

Thai chicken curry with potatoes and coconut milk 116

Meat

Champagne sausages with chestnut potato purée 138

Moroccan couscous 100

Potato-crust lamb with poached tamarillos 140

Tortitas de papa with chorizo and corn salsa verde 33

One-dish Meals

American baked potato with fluffy soufflé fillings 29

Indian dry potato curry in eggplant shells with yogurt 121

Indian potato curry with toor dhaal (yellow lentils) 122

Kuku sibzamini 90

Potato gratin with herbs, spinach, and cheese 61

Potato soufflé with mozzarella and almond-parsley pesto 62

Vegetable Accompaniments

Bay-roasted hasselbacks 72

Cajun potato wedges with spicy lemon and onions 37

Champ 74

Clapshot 74

Colcannon 74

Cracked new potatoes in coriander and red wine 59

Hash browns 38

Jansson's temptation 71

Pommes voisin 81

Potatoes dauphinoise 76

Potatoes en papillote scented with fresh herbs 22

Punchnep 74

Rumbledethumps 74

Swiss rösti 54

Pastry and Pasta

Chile potato tart with roasted tomatoes and garlic 30

Pasta and potatoes with macadamia pesto 130

Pizza con le patate 52

Potato gnocchi with walnut and arugula pesto 48

Baking and Sweet Things

Golden potato biscuits with parmesan and pancetta 86

Honey potato bread with saffron and a poppyseed glaze 85

Potato noodles with red cherry compote 82

index

mail-order sources

Adriana's Caravan
Brooklyn, NY
800-316-0820
Spices, condiments, and various other ingredients of every culture. Catalog/search service. Mail order only.

The CMC Company
PO Box 322, Avalon, NJ 08202
800-262-2780
Mexican, Asian, Indian, and other spices and ingredients. Catalog. Mail order only.

Dean & Deluca
560 Broadway, New York, NY 10012
800-221-7714
General gourmet ingredients. Retail and catalog mail order.

Foods of India
120 Lexington Avenue, New York, NY 10016
212-683-4419
Indian spices and ingredients. Retail and catalog mail order.

Integral Yoga, Natural Foods
229 West 13th Street, New York, NY 10011
212-243-2642
Natural and health food ingredients. Retail—no catalog, but items ordered by phone can be mailed.

Penzeys, Ltd.
PO Box 933, Muskego, WI 53150
414-679-7207
Wide range of international spices. Retail and catalog mail order.

Spice Merchant
PO Box 524, Jackson Hole, WY 83001
307-733-7811
800-551-5999
Indian and Asian spices. Retail and catalog mail order.

Zabar's
2245 Broadway, New York, NY 10024
212-787-2000
800-697-6301
General gourmet ingredients. Retail and catalog mail order.